TAKE TEN

TAKE TEN

daily bible reflections for teens

Maureen Gallagher
Jean Marie Hiesberger

saint mary's press

The publishing team included Brian Singer-Towns, development editor; Mary Koehler, permissions editor; Laurie Berg-Shaner, copy editor; Kimberly K. Sonnek, designer and typesetter; Andy Palmer, art director; manufacturing coordinated by the production services department of Saint Mary's Press.

Printed in the United States of America

ISBN 978-0-88489-821-4, Print
ISBN 978-1-59982-210-5, Digital

5031

Library of Congress Cataloging-in-Publication Data

Gallagher, Maureen, 1938-
    Take ten : daily Bible reflections for teens / Maureen
Gallagher, Jean Marie Hiesberger.
        p. cm.
ISBN 978-0-88489-821-4 (pbk.)
    1. Teenagers—Religious life. 2. Bible—Meditations.
3. Devotional calendars. I. Hiesberger, Jean Marie. II. Title.
BV4447.G35 2004
242'.63—dc22

                                                      2004012522

AUTHOR ACKNOWLEDGMENTS

Special thanks to the following teens, who were so helpful in reading and giving valuable suggestions for this work: John Bickimer, Julie Crowe, Tom Mulloy, Philip Noonan, Elaina Smith, Marisa Smith, and Tim Sullivan. Their insights and honesty were matched only by their generosity of time and good humor.

INTRODUCTION

Take Ten: that's what you're doing in these *Daily Bible Reflections for Teens*—taking ten minutes to do something simple and important! *Take Ten* is easy to use. Just open it to any date; you'll see that the page for each day follows the same simple format. It always begins with a Bible passage. This is followed by a commentary that connects the passage with your own life. Next is either a brief prayer or an action to make the Scripture passage active in your life. Finally, a suggestion for something more to read from *The Catholic Youth Bible*™ *(CYB)* is included, to help you go deeper into God's word today.

The Scripture passage is chosen from the Mass reading for the day, so that often it is the same one Catholic Christians all over the world are reading and listening to. Sometimes it is taken from the readings for a particular saint's feast day. You will be able to tell that from the title of the reflection. So, in a real sense, when you read the day's reflection, you are connecting with millions of people praying with the same Bible passage!

We suggest you use these reflections by first reading the Bible verse slowly and more than once, and then reflecting to see if a word or phrase jumps out at you or catches your interest. Let yourself be still for a minute or two with whatever thoughts come to you. Just sit quietly and let them sink in before you read the reflection.

Then read the short commentary. This paragraph often explains the Scripture passage a bit, but most important, it suggests a meaning or an application for your life. We make a difference as Christ's disciples by the way we live each day, and the commentary focuses on that. Sometimes the commentary poses a question, other times a challenge for you to think about. You'll have your own ideas, too. Write down your reaction if you wish. The important thing is to try each day in some small way to live the way Christ wants you to.

Prayer is the way we stay in touch with our God. The reflection ends with a prayer suggestion related to the message of the day. The prayer suggestions are there to help you talk with God. Read them and see if they say what you want to say. They are really prayer starters; it is hoped that they will inspire you to sit quietly with your thoughts and talk to God about whatever comes to mind.

If you use this reflection book with the *CYB,* you can expand your reflection even more. The articles in the *CYB* offer other insights into many of the daily reflection themes. The "To go deeper" sections will direct you to those articles. Take time to check out the recommended reading.

Some of the ideas on the pages of *Take Ten* come from teenagers like you. You'll also have your own ideas as you take ten minutes a day to nurture your relationship with God—a habit that will enrich your spiritual life.

God Bless You

The LORD bless you and keep you;
the LORD make his face to shine upon
   you, and be gracious to you;
the LORD lift up his countenance
   upon you, and give you peace.

(Numbers 6:24–26)

This blessing, which the Lord told Moses to give to God's people, is a wonderful way to start the year. The Lord is blessing you now and through the entire year, and the Lord will give you peace. Keeping this thought with you each morning will help you travel through the day and throughout the new year with confidence that you are not alone.

Dear Jesus, sometimes I forget that you want me to live a blessed life. Help me remember each day that staying close to you is the secret to life's blessings and peace.

▶ To go deeper: Read "God Bless You" near Numbers 6:22–27 in the *CYB*.

Who Is My Neighbor?

Those who say, "I love God," and
hate their brothers or sisters are liars.
. . . The commandment we have
from him is this: those who love God
must love their brothers and sisters
also.

(1 John 4:20–21)

Who is our brother and who is our sister? The author of
this letter is not talking just about our siblings or family
members. Nor is this quotation just about people we like
or who treat us well. It is about the people with whom we
rub shoulders every day, the people we see on the news,
those who live on other continents, and even people who
wish us ill or harm us. We may not feel love for them, but
we can at least not wish them harm, and we can pray for
them as well as ask God to help us in our attitude and
actions toward them.

*Heavenly Father, help me to see others with your eyes. Let me see
each person I meet today—even those I would normally turn away
from—as my brother or my sister.*

▶ To go deeper: Read "Understanding Love" near 1 John
4:7–21 in the *CYB*.

Childlike, Not Childish

> See what love the Father has given us,
> that we should be called children of
> God; and that is what we are.
>
> (1 John 3:1)

Imagine the most loving parent possible, someone who cares more for their son or daughter than for themselves and who will do anything for them. That is the kind of parent God is, a loving parent who created you and allowed Jesus to be killed for the salvation of the world. As one little boy said, "What a God!"

Although we are God's children, that doesn't mean we should act childish. We can be childish by always thinking of ourselves and praying only "gimme" prayers. Rather, we should be childlike. To be childlike is to feel awe and wonder. What is it about God, our loving parent, that is awesome to you?

In your own words, pray a prayer of gratitude and thanksgiving to the God who loves you so much and has given you so much.

▶ To go deeper: Read 1 John 2:29—3:24.

Saint Elizabeth Ann Seton

> As he went ashore, he saw a great crowd; and he had compassion for them, because they were like sheep without a shepherd; and he began to teach them many things.
>
> (Mark 6:34)

During his public life, Jesus was a teacher. He explained to all who would listen how much God loved them and how they should live their lives taking care of one another. Elizabeth Ann Seton, an American woman, did much the same. She was concerned about her children's education, so she started a school in Baltimore. She grew to have a great concern for the education of poor children, and started an order of nuns dedicated to teaching poor children and doing other works of charity. This saint didn't work miracles or have visions in her lifetime. She did what each of us is to do: live as well as we can the life we've been given.

Loving God, I want to follow the example of Saint Elizabeth Seton and live this day the way you want me to. Let me remember that I also teach through my actions and the values that guide my life.

▸ To go deeper: Read "Stand Up and Be Counted!" near Amos 8:4–8 in the *CYB*.

Loving My Brother and My Sister

Whoever says, "I am in the light,"
while hating a brother or sister, is still
in the darkness. Whoever loves a
brother or sister lives in the light, and
in such a person there is no cause for
stumbling.

(1 John 2:9–10)

The author of this letter reminds us that loving all God's children is essential to living in the light of Christ. That makes this Scripture passage a real challenge! Some people are just not as lovable as others. You've probably come across someone like this: the person who tries too hard to be liked, the person who can never stay on topic, or someone whose personal hygiene leaves something to be desired. Love means looking beyond human weaknesses to find the goodness God has placed in every human heart. When we do, our own capacity for goodness grows.

Dear Jesus, you never said it would be easy to be your follower. It is easier to love people who are far away than some of those I am with in my daily life. I need your help to put this challenge into practice.

▶ To go deeper: Read 1 John 2:7–17.

Epiphany

On entering the house, they saw the child with Mary his mother; and they knelt down and paid him homage. Then, opening their treasure chests, they offered him gifts of gold, frankincense, and myrrh.

(Matthew 2:11)

The three kings traveled far to see Jesus. In your life Jesus comes to you wherever you are. The Magi offered him homage and treasures. The homage you offer Christ is in your own prayer life and especially in your participation in the Eucharist, where he comes to you in the form of bread and wine. The treasure you offer is the kind of life you lead, the example you give as a disciple of Jesus Christ.

O God of generous gifts to me, accept this day and all that I do as homage to you and to your Son.

▶ To go deeper: Read "Jesus Brought the Good News of Salvation to People of All Races" near Matthew 2:1–12 in the *CYB*.

On the Mountain

> Immediately he made his disciples get into the boat and go on ahead to the other side, to Bethsaida, while he dismissed the crowd. After saying farewell to them, he went up on the mountain to pray.
>
> (Mark 6:45–46)

Jesus prayed in many different ways. This is one of several times when we are told that he went off by himself to pray. We, too, pray in many different ways. One of those is the way Jesus prayed here. Your "mountain" might be your room or a park bench or a chapel. It is just some-place where you can spend a little time alone and quiet. What happens next? You talk with your friend Jesus. Just have a conversation, telling him what's going on, what your concerns are, and what you need.

Dear Jesus, take me with you to the mountain and help me talk with God as you did. Then help me listen with an open heart.

▶ To go deeper: Read "The Making of a Prayer" near James 5:13 in the *CYB*.

Open Your Ears and Your Heart

> "Come and see a man who told me everything I have ever done! He cannot be the Messiah, can he?"
>
> (John 4:29)

This Samaritan woman, whom people looked down on, became a messenger of truth and wisdom. As a society we have come a long way in overcoming stereotypes and bigotry. Unfortunately, subtle forms of bigotry and discrimination still exist. This is especially true in regard to recent immigrants of other ethnic groups. But those peoples and their cultures will have something to teach us. Try to open your ears and your heart to those individuals today.

Holy Spirit, remind me during this day to listen to each person with the same respect and openness.

▸ To go deeper: Read "Stretch Me, Lord" near Acts of the Apostles 11:1–18 in the *CYB*.

Who, Me Preach?

That message spread throughout
Judea, beginning in Galilee after the
baptism that John announced: how
God anointed Jesus of Nazareth with
the Holy Spirit and with power; how
he went about doing good and healing
all who were oppressed by the devil,
for God was with him.

(Acts of the Apostles 10:37–38)

The Acts of the Apostles tells how the Apostles preached
the message of Jesus to people who were not yet followers
of Christ. Still today many people are not Jesus's followers.
The late bishop John Sullivan often said that Jesus doesn't
need to be here anymore to preach his message because
he has us here to do it. Most of us think we're not
preachers. Yet we really are—by the way we act and the
way we treat others. As the old saying goes, "What you are
shouts so loudly that I cannot hear what you say."

*Who are the people in your school or community who do not fully
know Jesus or his message? Try to think of some ways you might
share Jesus with them through your words and actions.*

▸ To go deeper: Read Saint Peter's speech in Acts 10:34–43.

God Listens to Our Needs

And this is the boldness we have in him, that if we ask anything according to his will, he hears us.

(1 John 5:14)

For what do you pray? for things? for good grades? for understanding? for patience? for the ability to cope with a situation? for courage? Perhaps you pray at some time for each of those things and more! Notice the condition in the Scripture verse, "if we ask anything according to his will." Sometimes the hardest part is figuring out what God's will is for us. So though we probably shouldn't expect God to step in and change a grade or get us a job, we can expect that the ways God answers our prayers—or doesn't answer our prayers—will help us to know his will better.

Dear Lord, I'll keep praying for the things that I believe are your will for me. And in the ways you answer my prayers, help me to know your will more clearly.

▸ To go deeper: Pray "The Peace Prayer of Saint Francis of Assisi" near Ephesians 6:10–17 in the *CYB*.

The Baptism of the Lord

Now when all the people were baptized, and when Jesus also had been baptized and was praying, the heaven was opened, and the Holy Spirit descended upon him in bodily form like a dove. And a voice came from heaven, "You are my son, the Beloved; with you I am well pleased."

(Luke 3:21–22)

None of us had such a dramatic and exciting baptism as Jesus did! But yours was just as important, whether you remember it or not. It was the beginning of your life as a Christian. And God just as truly said of you, "With you I am well pleased."

Learn about your own baptismal day—who was there, where it occurred, what it was like. Take a few minutes to think about times in your life when you know God would say, "With you I am well pleased."

Holy God, on the day of my baptism, I was brought into your family, the Body of Christ. Give me the strength to live a holy life that is pleasing to you.

▸ To go deeper: Read "Introducing John the Baptist" near Luke 3:1–20 in the *CYB*.

Good News

> "The time is fulfilled, and the kingdom of God has come near; repent, and believe in the good news."
>
> (Mark 1:15)

Sometimes it seems like we need to "repent" every day. It is not always easy to be the person God is calling you to be, and so sometimes you fail. The good news is that God's forgiveness is unlimited and help is always just a prayer away. The good news is that God believes in you even more than you do. Even more good news is that when you are faithfully responding to God's call, you are helping to bring about the Kingdom of God.

God of good news, you know that I want to do your will and that it is not always easy. I know you will both forgive me and help me do better if I acknowledge my sin. For this I praise you and thank you.

▶ To go deeper: Read "Called to Follow Jesus" near Mark 1:16–20 in the *CYB*.

Hearing His Voice

For we have become partners of Christ, if only we hold our first confidence firm to the end. As it is said,

> "Today, if you hear his voice,
> do not harden your hearts."

(Hebrews 3:14–15)

How do we hear God's voice? Taking even a few minutes each day to be still and think about the day ahead or the day just completed is a wonderful start. Quietly ask God to help you clear your mind as you think about the day's events. What could you do in your treatment of others that would help you be a "partner with Christ"? What did you do today for which you are thankful? Is there someone you want to treat better tomorrow than you did today? Put all this in God's hands. Then listen for God's voice. Do not harden your heart.

Start or continue a practice of quiet prayer early in the morning or before you go to bed. Consider keeping a journal of what you might be hearing God communicate to you.

▸ To go deeper: Read "Have a Heart" near Ezekiel 11:19–20 in the *CYB*.

How Should I Pray?

"You shall say, 'Speak, LORD, for your servant is listening.'"

(1 Samuel 3:9)

God was speaking to young Samuel, but Samuel didn't recognize God's voice. We may think of God speaking to people as something that only happened long ago or to certain special people. However, the Lord speaks to each of us. It may not be in a vivid dream or a voice we hear in the night. But God does speak to us—in the quiet of our hearts, in the Scriptures, through certain people who care about us and offer us wise advice, through nature, and in the circumstances of our lives, the things that happen to us. Our task is to have big ears to listen and quiet time to say, "Speak Lord, for your servant is listening."

Holy Spirit, help me to be as trusting as Samuel in hearing and responding to the voice of God. Make me aware of the many ways God can speak to me every day.

▶ To go deeper: Read "Eli Teaches Samuel How to Pray" near 1 Samuel 3:5 in the *CYB*.

Forgive Me

> He said to them, "Those who are well
> have no need of a physician, but those
> who are sick; I have come to call not
> the righteous but sinners."
>
> (Mark 2:17)

Jesus knew what it was like to live as a human being.
Amazingly, he struggled with the same things we do, so he
understands our sins and failures. And we all sin. We sin
in little ways and sometimes in big ways. What Jesus does
is stand by us and forgive us. What we must do is admit
our sins and ask Jesus for forgiveness. We also need to ask
those we've offended for forgiveness—and sometimes we
need to forgive ourselves.

*For what do you need forgiveness? Besides God's, whose forgiveness
do you need? What will you do about that?*

▶ To go deeper: Read "Getting Personal" near Mark 2:13–17
in the *CYB*.

Faithful Friends

> Then some people came bringing to
> him a paralyzed man, carried by four
> of them. And when they could not
> bring him to Jesus because of the
> crowd, they removed the roof above
> him; and after having dug through it,
> they let down the mat on which the
> paralytic lay.
>
> (Mark 2:3–4)

What wonderful friends the paralyzed man in this story
had! Who wouldn't want friends like them? The friends
we choose are a sign of who we are and what is important
to us. Friends have a great influence on how we think,
what we do, even who we are. Choosing friends who have
the same kind of values we have helps us live those values.
Befriending someone who wants to be like us is one way
we can give back what we've received from our own
family and friends. Look around at who you have as
friends. Thank God for the positive influence the people
you chose have on you.

*Dear Jesus, you know how important friends are in helping us live
as your disciples. Thank you for my friends, and help me to be a
positive influence on my friends in return.*

▶ To go deeper: Read "Faithful Friends" near Mark 2:8 in the
CYB.

Follow Wisely

As he was walking along, he saw Levi son of Alphaeus sitting at the tax booth, and he said to him, "Follow me." And he got up and followed him.

(Mark 2:14)

This is such an amazing scene, that Levi would just follow another person so easily. Sometimes people today do the same thing. They follow media stars, musicians, celebrities. They follow other people their own age who might be going in a different direction or doing something they've never tried. Sometimes when people follow others, they don't even recognize that's what they're doing. Who are the people you look up to and try to be like? What is it about them that attracts you?

Christ, light of the world, help me see clearly the path and the people to follow. Let me be strong enough not to follow those who would lead me away from you.

▶ To go deeper: Read more about who Jesus called in Mark 1:16–20, 2:13–17.

The Small Things Count

> For God is not unjust; he will not overlook your work and the love that you showed for his sake.
>
> (Hebrews 6:10)

Sometimes when we think of saints and holy people, we think of the people who do great or courageous or public acts. It is a mistake to think only of those. Small acts can make a big difference in a person's life. The person who receives an act of kindness can have their whole day, sometimes their whole life changed. Whether you offer a ride to someone, give someone a smile in the hallway, help another student understand an assignment he or she is struggling with, or pick up the house without being asked, God will not overlook your actions. And doing such things as a way of life is what makes someone a saint.

Dear God, help me to open my eyes today and discover where I can do an act of love for your sake.

▶ To go deeper: Read "Anchor of the Soul" near Hebrews 6:19–20 in the *CYB*.

Hunger

"For I was hungry and you gave me
food, I was thirsty and you gave me
something to drink."

(Matthew 25:35)

Many people in every town and city are hungry for real
food. There are many different ways to be hungry and
thirsty besides physical hunger. One person might hunger
for friendship, another might be hungry for peace and
quiet and time alone, another for help with solving a
problem. Christ calls us to respond to the hungers around
us, the physical hungers as well as the emotional and
spiritual hungers. But in order to respond, we have to take
time to notice the hungers around us.

*Look at the members of your family. For what do you think each of
them might be hungering? What could you do about it?*

▸ To go deeper: Read "You Did It to Me" near Matthew 26:2
in the *CYB*.

How Do I Look?

> But the LORD said to Samuel, "Do
> not look on his appearance or on the
> height of his stature, because I have
> rejected him; for the LORD does not
> see as mortals see; they look on the
> outward appearance, but the LORD
> looks on the heart."
>
> (1 Samuel 16:7)

How easy it is to judge someone by how they look! How
easy it is to criticize yourself because of how you look or
don't look. Here the Lord reminds us of what is important and what is lasting through life. Appearances will
fade. What is in the heart will not.

*Dear Jesus, you know what it feels like to be rejected and made fun
of. I want to look past physical appearances and pay more attention
to what is most important inside. Help me to do that today.*

▸ To go deeper: Read the story of David anointed as king, in
1 Samuel 16:1–13.

The Right Thing to Do

"Where you go, I will go;
   where you lodge, I will lodge."
(Ruth 1:16)

At great risk Ruth stayed with her mother-in-law, Naomi, when they were both left alone after the death of their husbands. She did this because it was the right thing to do. She volunteered to care for Naomi even when Naomi told Ruth to leave and return to her own family, who would take care of her. There are so many easier ways for you to volunteer your time than to do what Ruth did. We volunteer in works of service without expecting thanks just because it is the right thing to do. Remember Ruth as you think about where you will offer to volunteer.

Make a list of your skills and interests. Beside it make a list of places where you can volunteer in your community. Draw lines connecting your skills and interests to the places you might use them.

▸ To go deeper: Read "Service to the Poor and the Community" near Ruth, chapter 3 in the *CYB*.

Watch Over Me

"My sheep hear my voice. I know them, and they follow me. I give them eternal life, and they will never perish."

(John 10:27–28)

Chris didn't have parents like Ted's. Ted's parents had taken care of him since he was a baby, always supported him and encouraged him, and did their best to teach him to do the right thing. Chris, on the other hand, never had much support from his parents. He hid his loneliness by acting aloof and confident. It was only when he met an adult mentor who took real interest in his life that he began to understand the good shepherd parable. We don't like to feel helpless and dependent, but most people have those feelings occasionally. When you do, remember that like a good shepherd, Christ is there for you, too.

Jesus, my shepherd, help me to remember that I'm never all on my own. Even when I am not aware of it, you are there to guide and support me.

▸ To go deeper: Read "Jesus, the Good Shepherd" near John 10:16 in the *CYB*.

Courage

> Now Simon Peter was standing and
> warming himself. They asked him,
> "You are not also one of his disciples,
> are you?" He denied it and said, "I am
> not."
>
> (John 18:25)

Do you suppose Peter was scared? Do you suppose it was just so much easier to fit in with the crowd than to stand up for what he believed, to stand up for his friend? How understandable. What would have helped Peter to be stronger and not give in to that kind of pressure? To have courage in situations where we are tempted to give in as Peter did, we have to practice courage in small things. Obeying the speed limit when someone dares you to speed, or honoring your curfew when someone makes fun of you may seem unimportant, but doing those things builds character—the kind of character Peter needed that night.

God of friendship and understanding, help me practice courage in some small way today.

▸ To go deeper: To see how Peter is forgiven, read "The Humble Church" near John 21:15–19 in the *CYB*.

It Takes Conviction

"Other seed fell on rocky ground,
where it did not have much soil, and it
sprang up quickly, since it had no
depth of soil. And when the sun rose,
it was scorched; and since it had no
root, it withered away."

(Mark 4:5–6)

It may be easy to know the right thing to do, and to
believe you're going to do it. But sometimes when the
chips are down or when the pressure of friends tempts
you in the wrong direction, it is often easier not to follow
your conscience. Maybe it's leaving out an unpopular
person from your plans, maybe it's cheating a little on a
test or a paper, and maybe it's giving in to cigarettes or
drugs. Who and what helps you to be planted in "good
soil," that is, to have the deep convictions and courage
you need not to give in at times like that?

*Holy Spirit, give me the conviction to follow my conscience in doing
what is right, even when I am tempted not to.*

▸ To go deeper: Read "Jesus Teaches Us Through Stories!"
near Mark 4:1–34 in the *CYB.*

God Created Us All

> "'Truly I tell you, just as you did it to one of the least of these who are members of my family, you did it to me.'"
>
> (Matthew 25:40)

In the alley of a crowded Turkish bazaar, a dwarfed man who could hardly walk crept along carrying a bathroom scale. The merchants would leave their stands to give him a coin, stand on the scale, and weigh themselves. Actually they paid very little attention to what the scale read. They were just helping the man keep his dignity while offering a bit of help.

Who decides who is the "least" among us? No one you know carries a bathroom scale, but some people do carry the burden of being looked down on. Jesus is clear about how we should treat them.

O God who created all of us with love, help me remember those words of Jesus's today.

▶ To go deeper: Read "The Body of Christ" near 1 Corinthians 12:12–31 in the *CYB*.

Whose Faith Is It?

> I am reminded of your sincere faith, a
> faith that lived first in your grand-
> mother Lois and your mother Eunice
> and now, I am sure, lives in you.
>
> (2 Timothy 1:5)

Sometimes we have the faith that we do because it's our family tradition. Sometimes it begins with us. In either case, at a certain age we must make a choice and a decision about it for ourselves. It is an important decision, more important than what school to attend or what job to choose. Other people may even make fun of our choice to live a life of faith pleasing to God. But we have God's promise of grace to be with us in both choosing and living our faith. Just ask.

Dear Jesus, I ask for the gift of faith that I might believe in you and follow you all the days of my life.

▶ To go deeper: Read "Do Not Be Ashamed" near 2 Timothy 1:6–18 in the *CYB*.

Using Your Talents

He said to them, "Is a lamp brought in to be put under the bushel basket, or under the bed, and not on the lampstand?"

(Mark 4:21)

You were born with a certain personality and with certain talents and gifts. Some of them seem to grow and develop on their own. Some need to be practiced and developed. It is your responsibility to discover the gifts God has given you and not keep them hidden, as under a bushel basket. Sometimes friends and certain adults can help name your talents so that you can discover how to use those gifts of God during your lifetime.

Find someone you can talk to about the gifts she or he sees in you. Make a list of those gifts, and pray about how God might want you to use them.

▸ To go deeper: Read the parable of the talents in Matthew 25:14–30.

Saint Thomas Aquinas

"Other seed fell into good soil and brought forth grain, growing up and increasing and yielding thirty and sixty and a hundredfold."

(Mark 4:8)

The farmer in this parable had good crops when he planted the seed in soil that could make good use of it and help it grow. Saint Thomas Aquinas, the great philosopher and teacher, was "good soil" for God's word. He had gifts of great intelligence and an ability to write and teach, which he used so well he has influenced our Church for centuries. You, too, have been given gifts and talents to use during your lifetime. God is confident that you, like the farmer and like Saint Thomas Aquinas, are good soil and will use these gifts to the best of your ability.

Dear Jesus, like Saint Thomas Aquinas, help me to be good soil for your word. Be with me as your word grows within me and I discover how you wish me to use my gifts and talents.

▸ To go deeper: Read the entire parable of the sower in Mark 4:1–20.

Be Not Afraid

He woke up and rebuked the wind,
and said to the sea, "Peace! Be still!"

(Mark 4:39)

Jesus was asleep in the boat. His friends were awake and frightened by the windstorm that came up. The seas were rough. Imagine how they felt in their little boat, afraid and helpless. That is how you might feel sometimes, too. And the disciples show us exactly what to do when that happens. They take their anxieties and concerns to Jesus.

Who or what is it that causes you to be afraid? a person? a challenge you face? a fear of the unknown tomorrow? Place your fears in Jesus's care and ask him to be with you. Listen with your heart to his words, "Peace! Be still!"

Dear Lord, calm the fear inside me, just as you calmed the storm for the disciples when they asked you.

▸ To go deeper: Read "Be Not Afraid" near Joshua 1:5–9 in the *CYB*.

You Are Not Alone

They were all together in one place.
And suddenly from heaven there came
a sound like the rush of a violent
wind, and it filled the entire house
where they were sitting. Divided
tongues, as of fire, appeared among
them, and a tongue rested on each of
them. All of them were filled with the
Holy Spirit.

(Acts of the Apostles 2:1–4)

The Apostles now knew they had the Holy Spirit with
them, and so they weren't afraid anymore. They found
courage and strength that they didn't know they had.
Even though you don't walk around with a tongue of fire
on your head, the Holy Spirit is also with you. Remember
that when you feel challenged or uncertain. Remember
that when you are afraid or not sure what to do. "Come,
Holy Spirit" is a simple and important prayer for each of
us.

*Come, Holy Spirit, and fill me with courage and strength to
proclaim the good news of Jesus to the world.*

▶ To go deeper: Read "Send Us Your Spirit!" near Acts 1:24 in
the *CYB*.

Saint John Bosco

But Jesus . . . said to him, "Go home to your friends, and tell them how much the Lord has done for you, and what mercy he has shown you."

(Mark 5:19)

Those words of Jesus's might have been spoken by John Bosco to the young people he taught. John Bosco was an educator who started schools and eventually a religious order called the Salesians. Saint John Bosco believed in educating the whole person, not just the mind but also the body and the soul. Though he trained young people for the work world, he knew that what we do in our study, our play, and our work are all important. He said that all three of these need to be connected to our faith and to our understanding of Christ's love for us. How can you keep a balance of study, play, and work in your own busy life?

Saint John Bosco, you were so wise and helpful to young people during your life. Help me discover the same values and balance in my life that you taught your students.

▸ To go deeper: Read "Jesus Grows in Age and Wisdom" near Luke 2:41–52 in the *CYB*.

God's Family

Honor everyone. Love the family of
believers.

(1 Peter 2:17)

Who is my family? We can actually answer the question in
more ways than one. We think first of our immediate
family at home. Regardless of what it is like—one parent
or two, one sibling or many—it is our family. You may
also belong to other groups—close friends, teams—that
feel like family to you. You also have your Church family.
Catholics are never Catholic Christians alone. The Holy
Spirit brings us together as a community, a family of
believers. And just as in your biological family, you can be
either a passive member or a contributing member.

*Father of us all, thank you for the gift of the family of believers.
Help me to notice others in my faith community. Help me to
consider how I might be helpful to other members of that family.*

▶ To go deeper: Read "Part of the Family" near 1 Peter 2:9–17
  in the *CYB*.

Praise the Lord

Sing to God, sing praises to his name

. . . .

be exultant before him.

(Psalm 68:4)

One of the most important ways we honor people is by singing their praises. When we compliment people, several things happen. We share their goodness with others. We affirm them for who they are and what they do. And most important, we show that the quality or qualities they possess matter to us. God doesn't really need our praise. But *we* need to praise God. When we sing songs of praise and thanksgiving or participate in community prayer, we are saying that God's qualities are important for us. Just doing that helps us to be strong in those same qualities.

Give someone, especially someone who doesn't expect it, a compliment today. When you pray the Gloria at Mass, pay attention to the words of praise.

▶ To go deeper: Read "Black People Praise the Lord" near Psalm 68 in the *CYB*.

Have Faith!

"Daughter, your faith has made you well; go in peace, and be healed of your disease."

(Mark 5:34)

Faith is the hallmark of Jesus's ministry. Many of his miracles are based on the faith of the people requesting his help. Today we are bombarded by advertisements competing for our belief. People tell us to "eat this food and lose weight," "buy this car and be popular," "wear these clothes and be liked." Taking time to reflect on who we believe and what we believe is essential to healthy Christian spirituality. As Christians we are called to believe we are part of the Body of Christ and we share in the mission and ministry of Jesus. Our belief empowers us to try things that may seem impossible otherwise.

Holy Spirit, you show us how to believe and what to believe in. Sustain us now as we struggle to make a difference in the world under your guidance.

▶ To go deeper: Read about Jesus's healings in Mark 5:21–43.

Big Trouble

"I am in great distress; let us fall into
the hand of the LORD, for his mercy is
great."

(2 Samuel 24:14)

Sometimes we are "up to our neck in alligators." Our
troubles abound. Friends are mad. Parents don't understand. We are so far behind at work or school that it
seems hopeless. A significant relationship has ended. We
feel abandoned. We don't know where to turn. David felt
the same way, as indicated by the story from 2 Samuel.
However, David knew that no matter how difficult life
seems, no matter how much we have messed up, God is
merciful. God is always ready to forgive, to give us a fresh
start, to assure us that life is worth living.

*Dear Jesus, when life seems desperate, give me a new heart to begin
again. Help me always to be aware of your love and support in my
life.*

▸ To go deeper: Read "The Lord Is My Rock" near 2 Samuel
22:1–4 in the *CYB*.

Repent! Change Your Heart!

So they went out and proclaimed that all should repent.

(Mark 6:12)

To repent means to have a change of heart. Repentance beckons us not to be headstrong. It challenges us to begin again with a "clean heart." To be repentant, we need to look at what is important in our lives. What are our most cherished dreams? What relationships need attention?

Goals help us to follow through on our insights about repentance. Leaders often note that little is achieved without goals. Goals help us to succeed, to know where we are going. What goals do you wish to set so you can live with a clean heart?

Dear Jesus, you were always in touch with what your Father had in mind for you. Help me repent from my selfish ways so that I may see more clearly your direction in my life.

▸ To go deeper: Read "When the Good News Comes Calling" near Mark 6:6–13 in the *CYB*.

Dealing with the Death of a Friend

Herod himself had sent men who arrested John [the Baptist], bound him, and put him in prison on account of Herodias. . . . [Later] the king sent a soldier of the guard with orders to bring John's head.

(Mark 6:17,27)

When a friend dies because of a sickness, violence, or an accident, we are devastated. How could it happen? The person had so much to live for. It all seems so unfair. We are sad and angry. That's how the friends of John the Baptist felt.

Jesus was saddened by the death of John the Baptist. John was his cousin, his friend, his colleague in spreading the Good News. After John's death Jesus withdrew to a quiet place to have time for reflection (see Matthew 14:13). When we experience the loss of someone we love, it is good to take time alone to reflect on the meaning of the person's life and the person's impact on our life.

Holy Spirit, help me adjust to life without my good friend. Empower me to witness to the spirit and values by which my friend lived.

▶ To go deeper: Read "Growing Through Loss" near Lamentations, chapter 5 in the *CYB*.

Let Me Know Right from Wrong

"Give your servant therefore an understanding mind to govern your people, able to discern between good and evil."

(1 Kings 3:9)

When God asked Solomon what he wanted as king, Solomon asked for understanding and the ability to know right from wrong. Today we continue to need those gifts. How great it would be if we could truly understand those who do not agree with us, those who avoid us, and those who try to manipulate us. Sometimes we are so influenced by our peers that we forget we know the difference between right and wrong. A wise leader understands with the heart and mind the difference between right and wrong, and acts to do the right thing, even when those actions are unpopular.

Heavenly Father, strengthen me to be able to both understand with my heart and act from my conscience so that I can continue to be your effective disciple.

▸ To go deeper: Read "God, Give Me Wisdom!" near 1 Kings 3:4–15 in the *CYB*.

Whom Shall I Send?

> I heard the voice of the Lord saying,
> "Whom shall I send, and who will go
> for us?" And I said, "Here am I; send
> me!"
>
> (Isaiah 6:8)

God was looking for someone to send to his people to help them understand the faithfulness he expected from them. At first Isaiah was hesitant because he did not feel worthy of God's call, yet he ultimately responded by saying, "Send me." God needs us to make his presence known to others. We are God's arms, legs, and mouthpiece.

Which of your friends needs to hear that God loves them and wants them to be happy? Which friends need encouragement to turn their lives around so that they can grow closer to God? Besides words, what actions need to be taken so people can see God's presence?

Dear Jesus, help me to be your voice. Give me words that others will understand, even if I don't use your name. Let my actions reflect my words as I try to help others know your love for them.

▸ To go deeper: Read the story of Isaiah's call in Isaiah 6:1–8.

Touch and Healing

They laid the sick in the marketplaces,
and begged him that they might touch
even the fringe of his cloak; and all
who touched it were healed.

(Mark 6:56)

Have you ever considered how you can share in Jesus's
healing ministry? In almost all the stories of Jesus healing
people, there is the element of touch. Though we might
not have miraculous healing powers, through the gift of
touch, we have some power to help make people whole.
We give hugs when people are grieving to let them know
they are not alone. We give a pat on the back to let people
know we are with them and support them. Physical
therapists massage sore muscles and loosen them up,
enabling us to continue to play a game. We give "high
fives" as a sign of affirmation and congratulations.

*Holy Spirit, empower me to share in Jesus's healing ministry. Help
me to be aware of when the gift of touch can bring healing into
another person's life. Let me never misuse this great gift.*

▶ To go deeper: Read "Those Thickheaded Disciples" near
Mark 6:30–52 in the *CYB*.

Be Genuine!

"This people honors me with their
lips,
but their hearts are far from me."

(Mark 7:6)

Jesus abhorred hypocrisy. He had little time for "fakes,"
people who pretended to follow the law but who in
their hearts were far from being faithful. Jesus was less
concerned that people follow the law to the last detail
than that they love with their hearts. Sometimes it is easy
to go to church every Sunday and look like a Christian,
but when it comes to treating people as we would like to
be treated, we totally fail. Or we exhibit all the external
signs of being a Christian, but do not reach out to others
and care for them as Jesus calls us to do.

*Dear Jesus, enable me to live with integrity, incorporating your values
into my heart and making my life a genuine witness to your Good
News.*

▸ To go deeper: Read what Jesus has to say about holiness and
integrity in Mark 7:14–23.

Evil Comes from Within

"For it is from within, from the human heart, that evil intentions come: fornication, theft, murder, adultery, avarice, wickedness, deceit, licentiousness, envy, slander, pride, folly."

(Mark 7:21–22)

Sometimes when we see so much evil in the world, we think of it as external to us. Evil is out there somewhere. But in Mark's Gospel, Jesus tells us that evil comes from the heart. When a lot of people are selfish and refuse to share the goods of the earth, poverty happens. When people want to control others, war happens. When people see others as objects of pleasure, licentiousness (sexual promiscuity) happens. Evil begins in the heart. Injustice begins within people. What elements of greed, deceit, or licentiousness are you harboring in your heart? What can you do to eliminate them?

Dear Jesus, I wish to be a true follower of yours. Cleanse my heart from an inclination toward evil and help me create a more just world.

▸ To go deeper: Read "Sin's Source" near Mark 7:14–23 in the *CYB*.

Which Way
Is Your Heart Turned?

Then the LORD was angry with
Solomon, because his heart had
turned away from the LORD. . . .
[Solomon] did not observe what the
LORD commanded.

(1 Kings 11:9–10)

Solomon displeased God by following false gods. That
temptation is with us today. Some people make a god out
of material things—making demands on parents to buy
only designer clothes, to have the latest technology, or to
go on expensive vacations. In other words, material things
become a major focus of life. Other people may make
gods out of other human beings. These people have
undue influence on their followers, and the followers go
along with the mandates of the leader rather than God.
An example might be a gang leader or a popular person in
school whom people follow without question.

*Take time to think about people or things that might have an undue
influence over you. Are they keeping you from following Jesus with
your whole mind and heart? Are those your false gods?*

▶ To go deeper: Read "Solomon's Sin" near 1 Kings 11:1–8 in
the *CYB*.

Listen Up!

Then looking up to heaven, he [Jesus]
sighed and said to him, . . . "Be
opened." And immediately his ears
were opened, his tongue was released,
and he spoke plainly.

(Mark 7:34–35)

Jesus healed the deaf man. Sometimes we are "deaf"—
deaf to those struggling around us, deaf to the poverty in
our country and in other countries, deaf to the needs of
our parents and siblings. We don't hear the yearnings of
our peers to be accepted, the desire of others to be part of
our sphere of friends, and the longing of many to have the
same educational advantages we have.

We are called to "listen up" to the needs of those
around us. To do this means not focusing solely on our
own needs, but standing in the shoes of others and doing
what we can to make their lives happier.

*Heavenly Father, help me to "listen up" to the needs of other people
both near to me and far away. Help me to understand that
sometimes my lifestyle may contribute to poverty for others.*

▶ To go deeper: Read "Would You Do It?" near Exodus
22:21–27 in the *CYB*.

Happy Valentine's Day!

They ate and were filled; and they took up the broken pieces left over, seven baskets full.

(Mark 8:8)

The preceding quote is from the end of the story in which Jesus feeds four thousand people. It is a good reading for Valentine's Day because it reminds us that miracles happen when people give what they have to others. Valentine's Day is a commercial celebration of love, but it is rooted in the Gospel stories where Jesus reminds us to give our love to others. Think of the people whom you love. Remember to express your love for them today in some meaningful way. Remember, too, those unknown people who influence your life in many positive ways, from the people who grow your food to the people who collect your garbage.

Dear Jesus, enable me to see beyond the commercial glitter of Valentine's Day to discover the meaning of true love. Help me to express this love in a way that shows my deep appreciation.

▶ To go deeper: Read "The Miniature Gospel" near Matthew 22:34–40 in the *CYB.*

Blessed Are You
When You Are Excluded

"Blessed are you when people hate
you, and when they exclude you, revile
you, and defame you."

(Luke 6:22)

When we feel most miserable, Jesus is telling us that we
are blessed. How can that be? When I am not invited to a
party, when I am put down by my friends for living my
faith, then I am blessed? Jesus surprises us in the Beatitudes by pointing us to what is really important. He was
deserted by his friends when he was arrested. He was
insulted by those who did not share his values. He
basically was put to death by those who were threatened
by his very presence. When and why have you felt
excluded? When and why have you excluded others?

*Holy Spirit, strengthen me to withstand the pain of isolation and
insults. Give me the courage to never exclude or insult others.*

▸ To go deeper: Read "Justice for Those Who Are Poor" near
James 5:1–6 in the *CYB*.

Swallowed Up

> "Go at once to Nineveh, that great
> city, and cry out against it." . . . But
> Jonah set out to flee . . . from the
> presence of the LORD.
>
> (Jonah 1:2–3)

In the familiar story of Jonah, Jonah is called by God to
preach to the people of Nineveh, but he refuses and goes
in the opposite direction. The story tells of him being
swallowed by a big fish and kept in the fish's belly for
three days and three nights before being spit out upon the
shore. How often have we felt God's call in our heart? We
have an inkling of some good we should be doing. We see
some injustice. But we walk the other way. We don't get
involved. We don't want to leave our comfort zone with
our friends, our things, our lifestyle. Will it take something
dramatic for God to get our attention?

*Dear Jesus, empower me to respond to the things you challenge me to
do in my life. Give me courage to be a sign of your presence.*

▸ To go deeper: Read "Jesus and Jonah" near Jonah 2:2–10 in
the *CYB*.

God, Answer My Prayer

"Ask, and it will be given you; search, and you will find; knock, and the door will be opened for you."

(Matthew 7:7)

Matthew's Gospel makes it clear that if we pray, our prayers will be answered. But that is not always our experience. We prayed that we would ace an exam, that someone dear to us would be cured of cancer, that an out-of-work parent would quickly find a job—and none of it happened. God answers our prayers, but not always as we would like. In God's wisdom, sometimes what we are asking for is not the best thing for us. Or God's ability to answer may be dependent on the cooperation of other people. We must never stop asking God for what we need, but we must also trust that God will be with us through good times and bad times.

Heavenly Father, help me to understand that even when I do not get what I pray for, you are still with me, empowering me to be your faithful servant.

▶ To go deeper: Read "Supernatural Resources" near Wisdom of Solomon 19:22 in the *CYB*.

Never Too Late

> Have I any pleasure in the death of the
> wicked, says the Lord GOD, and not
> rather that they should turn from their
> ways and live?
>
> (Ezekiel 18:23)

Some people think God takes pleasure when we mess up.
However, Ezekiel makes it clear that God rejoices when
people who have been doing evil clean up their act and
remain faithful to God. In fact, Ezekiel goes so far as to
say that God forgets all the bad things the person has
done (see 18:22). Sin tends to paralyze people. They
feel badly because they have done wrong, but they are
tempted to wallow in their sin and they have no energy to
begin again. But God's grace is always there prompting
people to move forward, enabling them to seek forgiveness and begin again.

*Dear Jesus, when I sin I'm tempted to give up and even to get bogged
down in more sin. Help me to realize your presence and your love for
me. Forgive me for my lack of trust in you.*

▶ To go deeper: Read "Individuals Are Responsible for Their
   Behavior!" near Ezekiel 18:1–32 in the *CYB*.

Jealousy

> While they were at Hazeroth, Miriam
> and Aaron spoke against Moses
> because of the Cushite woman whom
> he had married, . . . and they said,
> "Has the LORD spoken only through
> Moses? Has he not spoken through us
> also?"
>
> (Numbers 12:1–2)

Miriam and Aaron had two problems. First, they were
clearly jealous of their brother, Moses. Second, they were
gossiping about Moses and criticizing him because he had
married a foreign woman. But those problems were all
connected. It's easy to look for fault and make unfounded
judgments about someone of whom we are jealous. In
fact, that's one of the primary signs of jealousy. When
have you been witness to or participated in such behavior?
What can you do to change that behavior?

*Dear Jesus, I want to be happy for the good fortune and gifts of
others, but sometimes I fail and feel jealous. Help me to overcome
such feelings and to not participate in gossip and criticism.*

▸ To go deeper: Read "The Jealousy of Miriam and Aaron"
  near Numbers, chapter 12 in the *CYB*.

What Do You See?

> Jesus came and touched them, saying, "Get up and do not be afraid." And when they looked up, they saw no one except Jesus himself alone.
>
> (Matthew 17:7–8)

This scripture passage is at the end of the story in which Jesus is transformed—his clothes and body becoming radiant as light. The disciples were awed in seeing Jesus as his heavenly Father saw him. They had new insights into his relationship with God. If we can see through God's eyes in our daily relationships, we might also understand things differently. A sibling who is always borrowing your "stuff" can irritate you. But you can also see the situation transformed, recognizing that your sibling looks up to you and wants to be like you.

Holy Spirit, help me to see the things in my life transformed through God's eyes and to respond with new understanding.

▶ To go deeper: Read "The Transfiguration" near Matthew 17:1–13 in the *CYB*.

Stop Judging

"Be merciful, just as your Father is merciful. Do not judge, and you will not be judged; do not condemn, and you will not be condemned."

(Luke 6:36–37)

How easy it is to judge others. The criteria we often use include looks, dress, academic achievement, personality, athletic skill, and so on. We come to shallow decisions about who is in and who is out. We disassociate from those who do not wear designer clothes or who are overweight. Judging and condemning others is not the good news of the Gospel. Reaching out to those who seem to be excluded, partnering with those who have a hard time in school, and fostering an inclusive spirit are ways to practice God's acceptance.

How are you judgmental of others? What secret or obvious prejudices do you carry in your heart or act out in your choice of those you associate with?

▸ To go deeper: Read Luke 6:37–42 and think about how it applies to your life.

Don't Lord It Over Others!

> Do not lord it over those in your charge, but be examples to the flock.
>
> (1 Peter 5:3)

Jesus asked Peter to be the first leader of the community that came to be known as the Church. In this letter attributed to Saint Peter, he gives other leaders the advice not to "lord [their leadership] over" others. True Christian leaders do not act out of pride and arrogance, but out of service and humility.

Today we might not be assigned a flock as such, but we each have groups of people with whom we relate. Lording our knowledge or position over others will not witness to them the love of Christ. But working with others, listening, caring, and taking responsibility are all ways to witness to true Christian leadership.

Dear Jesus, help me to exercise true Christian leadership. Assist me in making my life one that reflects your values and inspires others to follow you.

▸ To go deeper: Read "Living Gospel Values Even if It Demands Suffering" near 1 Peter 3:8–15 in the *CYB*.

Having an Awful Day

Be gracious to me, O LORD, for I am
> in distress;
>> my eye wastes away from grief,
>> my soul and body also.

(Psalm 31:9)

Each of us has bad days. Sometimes we cannot even talk about what made our day go so badly. At other times we know why we are so miserable. It could be the test we failed, the free throw we missed that caused our team to lose the tournament, the invitation we did not get, an argument with a parent or a friend. The psalmist, David, had those same experiences. In the psalm he acknowledges his misery and despair and asks God to look graciously on him. God does not take away the pain and anguish, but God makes his presence known and helps David see the light at the end of the tunnel.

Heavenly Father, when I am down and feel on the brink of despair, give me strength to see your light in my life.

▸ To go deeper: Read all of Psalm 31.

Rooted in God

Blessed are those who trust in the
    Lord,
. . . .
They shall be like a tree planted by
    water,
. . . .
It shall not fear when heat comes,
. . . .
    and it does not cease to bear fruit.
             (Jeremiah 17:7–8)

Jeremiah is reminding us that we need to be rooted in
God to be able to endure the many disappointments,
sufferings, and hardships of life. Being rooted in God
gives us the strength and endurance to weather the storms
that come our way. To be rooted in God, we need to make
a conscious effort to reflect on God's presence in our
lives, pray for God's guidance, and act in a way that
reflects Christ's values and teachings. To be rooted in God
also means to be connected to the Body of Christ, the
Church.

*Holy Spirit, help me to be rooted in God through my prayer, the
sacraments, and my involvement in the Church. Remind me daily
that Jesus Christ is my friend and savior.*

▸ To go deeper: Read "Children and Green Trees" near
  Jeremiah 17:1–3 in the *CYB.*

Don't Be a Hypocrite!

> "So whenever you give alms, do not sound a trumpet before you, as the hypocrites do in the synagogues and in the streets, so that they may be praised by others."
>
> (Matthew 6:2)

No one appreciates someone who is always bragging about his or her accomplishments. The most effective way to serve others is quietly, so no one knows who did what good deed. Many people give anonymous gifts so they will not be the center of attention. Yet it is tempting to be boastful about all we have done and accomplished. But Jesus' point is that the true motivation for our generosity should be to please God, not to impress other people. For in truth, in giving to others, we are only giving back to God what God has first given us.

Heavenly Father, you have given me many gifts, and I want to use them for your glory. Strengthen me to use what I have for others in a quiet, respectful way.

▸ To go deeper: Read "Sacrificial Giving" near Mark 12:41–44 in the *CYB*.

Stop Comparing

"Son, you are always with me, and all that is mine is yours. But we had to celebrate and rejoice, because this brother of yours was dead and has come to life; he was lost and has been found."

(Luke 15:31–32)

Jesus, in the parable of the prodigal son, reminds us that celebration is called for when a sinner mends her or his ways. Yet the faithful son objected to his father's lavish celebration for the wayward son. Sometimes we share the older brother's objection. We wonder what is so great about being sober for thirty days when we have never engaged in underage drinking. We resent the attention given to a younger sibling for succeeding in a difficult task when we never had any trouble doing the same thing. At those times it is good to remind ourselves that we seem to have an extra "gene" for self-righteousness.

Dear Jesus, help me to rejoice when others succeed at something I find very easy. Empower me to understand all the challenges with an open heart and mind.

▶ To go deeper: Read "God's Limitless Love" near Luke 15:11–32 in the *CYB*.

Do the Unexpected

"How is it that you, a Jew, ask a drink of me, a woman of Samaria?"

(John 4:9)

In the story of the woman at the well, Jesus breaks with the mores of his time and talks to a Samaritan woman. Jews did not associate with Samaritans. Men did not talk to women in public. Jesus's perspective was different. He saw all people as equally loved by God. In our time we live in a culture of discrimination that is not altogether different from Jesus's time. In school cafeterias we see people sitting in groups where others do not feel welcome. At work we hear racial slurs. We see people harassed because of their ethnic background. It is hard to break down those barriers, but it can be done—one person at a time.

Dear Jesus, give me the courage to reach out to people who are discriminated against. Let me learn from them so that I can see them from your perspective—as loved by God.

▸ To go deeper: Read "Why Are the Disciples Surprised?" near John 4:1–42 in the *CYB*.

Leave Everything?

> After this he went out and saw a tax collector named Levi, sitting at the tax booth; and he said to him, "Follow me." And he got up, left everything, and followed him.
>
> (Luke 5:27–28)

But how can we leave everything? our friends? our family? our future? When Jesus calls us to leave everything, he is calling us to make sacrifices and set priorities. If our friends lead us to discount the values and commandments of Jesus, we are to leave them. The call to follow Jesus is a call to make sure the commandments of Jesus—to love God and neighbor—are what rule our lives, not other people, not materialism, and not secular culture. Jesus asks us not to get immersed in the places, people, and events of the world so that we forget what we are really about.

Dear Jesus, I do want to follow you. Inspire me to be a faithful disciple, to leave everything that is taking me away from your mission to build a more just world.

▸ To go deeper: Read "Here I Am, Lord!" near Isaiah 6:1–13 in the *CYB*.

Top Priority

"It is written,
  'Worship the Lord your God,
    and serve only him.'"

(Luke 4:8)

We are often tempted to make something or someone other than God the focus of our lives. Sometimes we live for material things—designer clothes, a sports car, the latest in technology. At other times our total attention is centered on other people—our peers or a special friend. We live and breathe what others are doing and what we will do with them. God wants us to have friends and the material things we need to sustain our life; those are blessings from God. But when things and people become the center of all our energies, we have made them our "gods."

Holy Spirit, in a world that is permeated with materialism and consumerism, give me the gift of right judgment to help me not be swept up in acquiring more and more things.

▸ To go deeper: Read "Free . . . to Be Tempted" near Luke 4:1–13 in the *CYB*.

You Are Holy

> Speak to all the congregation of the
> people of Israel and say to them: You
> shall be holy, for I the LORD your
> God am holy.
>
> (Leviticus 19:2)

God is holy. You are created by God and in the image of
God. You are baptized into the life of Christ. These things
also make you holy. But what do you need to do to
continue to live as a holy person? Holy people continue to
grow in their faith, and their faith makes a difference in
how they live their lives. Part of how we do this is by
continuing to learn about our faith and participating in
the great gifts of the sacraments, especially the Eucharist.
In that way we become a fuller part of a community that
walks in faith each day.

*Thank you, Creator God, for making me in your image. I will try,
today and all during this Lent, to remind myself every day that you
created me to be a holy person.*

▸ To go deeper: Read "The Covenant Laws" near Leviticus,
chapter 2 in the *CYB*.

A Beautiful Vision

> For as the rain and the snow come
>   down from heaven,
>   and do not return there until they
>   have watered the earth,
> making it bring forth and sprout,
>   giving seed to the sower and bread
>   to the eater.
>
> (Isaiah 55:10)

Isaiah describes a world in which no sin or injustice or unkindness exists, a world in which people truly care for one another. That is hard to imagine some days when we look around at our world. But each of us can do something in our own corner of the world to make this vision a reality. Your words and actions can be like the rain that brings goodness to the soil. You can help make Isaiah's beautiful vision a bit more real.

Dear Jesus, help me to be your hands and feet in bringing about your vision for the world—a world in which people love each other to the fullest and do not sin.

▶ To go deeper: Read "The Optimism of Third Isaiah" near Isaiah, chapter 56 in the *CYB*.

Saint Katherine Drexel

"Be strong and bold; have no fear or dread of them, because it is the LORD your God who goes with you; he will not fail you or forsake you."

(Deuteronomy 31:6)

Saint Katherine Drexel certainly didn't think of herself as strong and bold when she was your age. Growing up in a wealthy Philadelphia family, she was interested in getting her ears pierced and in her family's private railroad car. But her mother fed poor people several times a week and her father prayed a half hour each day. Before her life ended, Katherine had given up her millions of dollars and begun schools for Native Americans and African Americans, including Xavier University in New Orleans.

What practices do you see in your family and friends that respond to the needs of poor people? What practices do you see that develop a deeper relationship with God?

▶ To go deeper: Read "A Prayer Against Prejudice" near Joshua, chapter 2 in the *CYB*.

Saint Casimir

Those who are wise understand these
    things;
    those who are discerning know
        them.
For the ways of the LORD are right,
    and the upright walk in them,
    but transgressors stumble in them.

(Hosea 14:9)

A teenager leading an army? That is part of the life story of Saint Casimir. He became a conscientious objector after seeing how poorly his soldiers were treated. A serious and prayerful young man, he decided never again to be involved in war, and was punished by his father for this with three months' confinement. Though he reigned briefly as ruler of Poland, he died at the age of twenty-three of lung trouble. This young man is the patron saint of two countries: Poland and Lithuania.

God of all graces, help me, like Casimir, to have the courage to live out my convictions even when others scorn me. Help me, like this young saint, to stay close to you in prayer.

▶ To go deeper: Read "Nonviolent Resistance" near 2 Maccabees, chapter 8 in the *CYB*.

Come Back

"Come, let us return to the LORD;

. . . .

. . . let us press on to know the
    LORD;
  his appearing is as sure as the dawn;
he will come to us like the showers,
  like the spring rains that water the
    earth."

(Hosea 6:1–3)

It is easy to stray from the Lord. Life is filled with
distractions and with people and events that call to us and
take us down paths that God would not have us travel.
But, wonderfully, our loving God is always waiting for us,
no matter how far away we've strayed or for how long
we've neglected him. As the prophet Hosea says, we know
this as surely as the sun will rise again and the spring rains
will come. Knowing this, what will you do today to grow
in your relationship with God?

*Holy Spirit, you are always ready to guide us back to God. Give me
the nudge I need today to take time to nurture my relationship with
you.*

▸ To go deeper: Read "Unconditional Faithfulness" near
  Hosea 3:1–3 in the *CYB*.

Pray for My Enemies?

"You have heard that it was said, 'You shall love your neighbor and hate your enemy.' But I say to you, Love your enemies and pray for those who persecute you, so that you may be children of your Father in heaven."

(Matthew 5:43–45)

This is sure a hard saying! Love my enemies? When I look at those who gossip about me, exclude me, make fun of me, or worse, I know that Jesus was calling special people to be his followers because it isn't easy to love our enemies. I also know that Christ is with me today, helping me to live this hard saying. I need only ask for Christ's help.

God who loves all of us, sinners and saints, be with me today as I try to make a special effort to live these words of Jesus's. Help me at least to pray for those whom I resent, dislike, or even hate.

▶ To go deeper: Read "Christians and Revenge" near Matthew 5:38–48 in the *CYB*.

Perpetua and Felicity, Martyrs

Keep on doing the things that you
have learned and received and heard
and seen in me, and the God of peace
will be with you.

(Philippians 4:9)

Saint Paul urged the Philippians not to worry over the
things that make us anxious, but rather to rejoice and let
God's peace fill us. Two early Christian women, Perpetua
and her slave Felicity, are the ultimate examples of that
attitude. Even though Perpetua had recently given birth
and Felicity was pregnant, they went to prison rather than
say they weren't Christians. Perpetua's father begged them
to lie rather than go through such suffering as they did.
Eventually they were beheaded at the public games. They
went to the amphitheater joyfully, knowing they were on
their way to heaven.

*Dear Jesus, grant me the gift of being joyful in all circumstances,
confident that you are in control of my ultimate destiny no matter
what happens to me.*

▸ To go deeper: Read Philippians 4:4–14.

It's Not Always Easy

"Do not judge, and you will not be judged; do not condemn, and you will not be condemned. Forgive, and you will be forgiven; give, and it will be given to you."

(Luke 6:37–38)

For some people this may be the most difficult part of Jesus's message. It seems to be part of our human nature to judge others, to gossip and criticize, and even to condemn people we don't like or with whom we disagree. And how very hard it can be to forgive! But just because these are hard sayings, it doesn't mean we are excused from trying to follow them.

O God of infinite forgiveness, I will try again to forgive even after I fail to do so. I know you are pleased with my efforts to be a forgiving person, even if they are imperfect at times.

▶ To go deeper: Read "The Reunion Dinner" near Luke 7:1–10 in the *CYB*.

Saint Frances of Rome

"The greatest among you will be your servant."

(Matthew 23:11)

Saint Frances, a wealthy young woman, had many responsibilities as a wife and mother. But when the plague struck Rome, she used all her money and sold her possessions to buy whatever the sick needed. In its cruelty the sickness killed two of her six children. Afterward this laywoman continued serving the poor for the rest of her life and even started a special community of women devoted to her cause.

It is clear that Frances was a servant. She didn't start with anything too dramatic, just visiting people in hospitals. So don't think you have to be a servant in dramatic ways and therefore miss the opportunities around you.

In what ways are you able to be of service to other people? To whom else in your life could you be of service?

▸ To go deeper: Read "Introducing Phoebe and Junia" near Romans 16:1–16 in the *CYB*.

You Want What from Me?

[Jesus] said to her, "What do you want?" She said to him, "Declare that these two sons of mine will sit, one at your right hand and one at your left, in your kingdom."

(Matthew 20:21)

Wow, what a favor "Mrs. Zebedee" wanted! Truly she didn't realize what she was asking. But Jesus listened kindly and patiently, and then explained what her favor meant and why he couldn't give her what she wanted. His response is a good model for us when someone wants something from us. No matter how outrageous the favor might be, try to stop and remember how Jesus treated the mother of these friends of his when she asked an impossible favor.

Dear Jesus, I want to remember to listen patiently to the person who wants something from me even if I think it's unreasonable. Let me remember how you treated the mother of your friends.

▶ To go deeper: Read "True Greatness" near Matthew 20:20–28 in the *CYB*.

The Outsider

"'I was a stranger and you welcomed me.'"

(Matthew 25:35)

Have you ever been the one who is the outsider or the stranger? Perhaps you've gone to a new school, joined a new group or team, or been the new person at your job. You know how it feels. This should make us sympathetic toward other people who are going through the experience of being the new person. Yet here's another twist: Jesus is saying that he is that person. And you are the person who has the choice to welcome or ignore him, to help him or leave it to others. How will you treat him the next time you meet?

O God of welcome, help me to welcome the stranger as I'd want to be welcomed. Help me to remember these words of Jesus's.

▶ To go deeper: Read "Be Kind to Strangers" near Genesis 19:1–11 in the *CYB*.

Dad Likes You Better!

> But when his brothers saw that their father loved him more than all his brothers, they hated him, and could not speak peaceably to him.
>
> (Genesis 37:4)

This sentence tells just the beginning of what Joseph's jealous brothers did to him in this story of sibling rivalry and family jealousy! Even in today's families, such feelings are not unusual. However, the wonderful lesson in Joseph's story is that he was able to forgive and love his brothers after what they did to him. Forgiveness is the result of both grace and hard work.

Of whom are you jealous? If you have siblings, what kinds of jealousies come between you and them? Ask God for the grace to rejoice in other people's gifts and to recognize your own unique gifts.

▶ To go deeper: Read "Introducing Joseph" near Genesis, chapter 37 in the *CYB*.

Lost and Found

> "Which one of you, having a hundred
> sheep and losing one of them, does
> not leave the ninety-nine in the
> wilderness and go after the one that is
> lost until he finds it?"
>
> (Luke 15:4)

It might seem that in a flock of a hundred sheep, a single sheep wouldn't even be missed, let alone be important enough for a search. Not so, Jesus says. Each and every person is that valuable to God. Yet sometimes we have a hard time believing that God loves us like that and looks for us when we stray. Take to the Lord your loneliness or your feelings of guilt when you stray from how you want to behave. Place in his care your fears and your feeling of being lost and ask for comfort and guidance. The shepherd is there for you.

Dear Jesus, sometimes I feel so far from you and your Father. I do not feel worthy of your love and attention. In those times, break through the walls of pain and guilt I've built so I might know your love again.

▸ To go deeper: Read "Lost and Found" near Luke 15:1–7 in the *CYB*.

It's Not Your Job

> "Let anyone among you who is
> without sin be the first to throw a
> stone at her."
>
> (John 8:7)

Someone is being judged by others. These others have decided she's done wrong, and they're going to get her for it. Jesus says that's not up to them to do. Most people do not take it upon themselves to punish someone else for doing wrong. However, most people *do* find it easy to judge others. Jesus says not to condemn another person in our mind or our heart. Gossiping, criticizing, judging—that's not our job.

Dwell in me, Holy Spirit, so my life will reflect your fruits of charity, kindness, and humility when I am tempted to judge other people.

▶ To go deeper: Read "Divine Compassion" near John 8:2–11 in the *CYB*.

You Are Not Alone

"And the one who sent me is with me;
he has not left me alone."

(John 8:29)

Loneliness is sometimes the greatest cross a person has to
bear. To feel separated, to feel you have no one to confide
in, to feel like a little boat alone on a rough sea can be a
dreadful experience. These words Jesus used to describe
his relationship with his heavenly Father are just as true
for you. God's presence to you is as real as the people
who may seem to pass you by. You are not alone. When
you feel you are, be still and talk with the God who has
not abandoned you.

*O God, listen to the longing in my heart. Help me not to feel sorry
for myself but to gain the insights I need to deal with my loneliness.
Knowing you are here with me gives me comfort and strength.*

▶ To go deeper: Read "Alone!" near Mark 15:33–34 in the
CYB.

A Gift of Freedom

> Then Peter came and said to him,
> "Lord, if another member of the
> church sins against me, how often
> should I forgive? As many as seven
> times?" Jesus said to him, "Not seven
> times, but, I tell you, seventy-seven
> times."
>
> (Matthew 18:21–22)

Have you ever been so angry or upset with someone else
that it was all you could think of? When you forgive
someone, you give yourself a gift. It is the gift of a free
heart and a free mind, no longer carrying the burden of
resentment or hatred. The other person may not even
know you have forgiven them, or even know that they
hurt you or wronged you. But you know you felt
wronged, and you know you're now free.

*Slowly pray three times the part of the Our Father that begins,
"Give us this day our daily bread . . ."*

▸ To go deeper: Read "Forgive Us Our Debts" near Matthew
18:21–35 in the *CYB*.

Saint Patrick

We had courage in our God to declare
to you the gospel of God in spite of
great opposition. For our appeal does
not spring from deceit or impure
motives or trickery.

(1 Thessalonians 2:2–3)

There are so many legends and myths about Saint Patrick
that it is difficult to know who he really was. But some of
what is known to be true is that he was captured and sold
as a slave in Ireland when he was a teenager. He endured
cold and hunger as a shepherd during that time, but
escaped, probably to France, where he was educated. As
a convert Patrick had a dream to bring Christianity to
Ireland, which, over many years of hard work, he did.
Patrick was humble but determined in carrying out his
life's dream.

*What dream do you have for your future? What do you want to
accomplish? Pray to Saint Patrick to help you discover your life
mission and carry it out with determination and humility..*

▸ To go deeper: Read "Doing the Right Thing" near 1 Thessalonians 2:1–2 in the *CYB*.

Me Sing?

Sing to the LORD;
  praise the LORD!
For he has delivered the life of the
      needy
    from the hands of evildoers.

(Jeremiah 20:13)

Did you ever feel so happy that you could shout? Was it an A on a paper? a close football game? a student council election? A little boy in Michigan shot out into the schoolyard, screeched to a halt, threw his arms in the air, and shouted, "Praise the Lord for this beautiful day!" Not many of us have the spontaneity of young children, but we can and do publicly praise and thank the Lord in many ways. One way is lifting our voices in prayer and song at church. Though this may not always feel comfortable, it is an ancient tradition with roots in the Old Testament. God doesn't expect beautiful voices. God is praised by all the voices.

Sing along courageously the next time you're in church, or at least follow and pray the words as they're sung. Join your voice in the spoken prayers.

▶ To go deeper: Read "Enthusiastic Praise!" near Revelation, chapter 5 in the *CYB*.

Saint Joseph

> Then Joseph got up, took the child and his mother by night, and went to Egypt, and remained there until the death of Herod.
>
> (Matthew 2:14–15)

He was just an ordinary young man growing up in a village, planning to be a carpenter and raise a family. Yet because of his commitment to God and Mary, he found himself unexpectedly having to leave to take Mary and her unborn child to a safe haven. Imagine having to leave not just your friends and your town but your country so that your child would survive. Today parents like Joseph flee their country because of persecution or incredible poverty that is killing their children. Many of them come to our country. Do we welcome them as we would Joseph, Mary, and Jesus?

Find out where the immigrants are in your town or city. What can you do to ease their pain and help them adjust here? Even a little help is appreciated.

▸ To go deeper: Read "Jesus' Family Lives as Immigrants!" near Matthew 2:13 in the *CYB*.

Who's Better?

"'God, I thank you that I am not like other people: thieves, rogues, adulterers, or even like this tax collector. I fast twice a week; I give a tenth of all my income.'"

(Luke 18:11–12)

Jesus used this man as an example of exactly how *not* to act. The poor fellow was doing good things; he was tithing generously and he was fasting. The problem, of course, was that he was filled with pride and self-congratulations at how good he was. We tend to fall into the same trap. We may congratulate ourselves for doing well in school, avoiding alcohol and other drugs, and obeying our parents and teachers. But we also look down on those who haven't lived up to those standards. Do the right thing, Jesus says, but do it quietly. Your good works are between you and God.

O God who loves the humble, remind me to do good deeds each day and also to never put others down. Jesus made it clear that I do not need to compare myself to others to deserve your love. I already have it.

▸ To go deeper: Read the entire story of the Pharisee in Luke 18:9–14.

I Am With You

I am the LORD, I have called you in
    righteousness,
  I have taken you by the hand and
    kept you.

(Isaiah 42:6)

Picture a child firmly holding the hand of a parent or an
older person. Imagine how each of them feels. The child
feels secure and loved. The adult feels protective and
caring. That is the image God uses with his servant. Isaiah
was God's servant, and so are you. God is saying to each
of his servants: "There is no need to be afraid. I am
beside you. I will stay with you." That security is to make
you feel not childish but strong. It means you can afford
to take the risk of doing the right thing even when the
crowd goes in the opposite direction.

*Think of a time when you didn't do the right thing because of peer
pressure. Picture yourself doing the right thing the next time,
repeating three times, "I have taken you by the hand and kept you."*

▶ To go deeper: Read "The Servant Songs" near Isaiah 42:1–7
  in the *CYB*.

I Feel Jealous

So the chief priests planned to put Lazarus to death as well, since it was on account of him that many of the Jews were deserting and were believing in Jesus.

(John 12:10–11)

Some people seem to have it all: money, a nice car, good looks, friends. They seem to get all the breaks, are popular, and don't seem to have to work for it. In the Gospel passage, the high priests' jealousy of Jesus's popularity with the people was even leading them to plot Lazarus's murder. To counteract feelings of jealousy, don't presume to know what other people's lives are really like—things can be very different from what they seem. Also, recognize the blessings you have without comparing them to other people's blessings. Finally, talking about it with your friend Jesus can be the best remedy for jealous feelings.

Jesus, I don't want to feel jealous. Help me to understand that I have all the gifts I need to live out your calling for me. Help me to see my own blessings and not just the other person's.

▸ To go deeper: Read about Lazarus in John 11:28–44.

Healing Ministry

> Jesus said to him, "Stand up, take your mat and walk." At once the man was made well, and he took up his mat and began to walk.
>
> (John 5:8–9)

This is a wonderful ending to the story. Just imagine, this man had been sick for thirty-eight years. Not all stories of sickness and pain have such happy endings, of course. Some people live with serious illness or disabilities their whole lives. Some endure terrible suffering at different times in their lives. Elderly people also often deal with the pain of loneliness. We can be God's hands and voice for those people. Consider joining a group at school or church that visits people with disabilities or elderly people in your community.

Thank you, God, for the gift of my health. Give me the courage to be with people who are ill or lonely. Help me to take your joy and comfort to them.

▸ To go deeper: Read about Jesus's healing ministry in John 5:1–18.

Do As I Have Done

"So if I, your Lord and Teacher, have washed your feet, you also ought to wash one another's feet. For I have set you an example, that you also should do as I have done to you."

(John 13:14–15)

The Apostles' feet were dirty from walking in open sandals on dusty roads and paths. Imagine Jesus kneeling down and washing each Apostle's feet before they ate. What he did was an act of great love and service.

Natalie works in a nursing home, and sometimes when she bathes the residents and patients, it is not a pleasant task. Some are cranky, some smell bad, and some are in pain when she moves them. Natalie tries to remember this story about Jesus when she feels impatient.

Holy Spirit, you call us to see each person as sacred. So even the most basic—and possibly unpleasant—acts of service for another person are not demeaning acts but sacred acts.

▶ To go deeper: Read "Jesus Models Service to Others" near John 13:1–17 in the *CYB*.

The Crucifixion

So Jesus came out, wearing the crown
of thorns and the purple robe. Pilate
said to them, "Here is the man!"
When the chief priests and the police
saw him, they shouted, "Crucify him!
Crucify him!"

(John 19:5–6)

Around this time in the Church year, we celebrate the
suffering and death of Jesus on Palm Sunday and Good
Friday. It is important, at least once a year, to meditate on
this true story. It is an amazing story of courage and great
love on the part of Jesus, of mob anger and violence, and
of a lack of courage by Pilate. It is a major part of our
story as Christians. Sit quietly and read the whole thing as
though you have never heard it before. Feel the fear of the
disciples, the calmness and commitment of Jesus, the
anger of the crowd, and Pilate's wavering over what to do
with Jesus.

*Make a commitment to read the story of Jesus's Passion (suffering)
during Holy Week. Pray the prayer that is in your heart when
you've finished the story.*

▶ To go deeper: Read the story of Jesus's Passion and death in
John 18:1—19:42.

You Will Live Forever

> But the angel said to the women, "Do not be afraid; I know that you are looking for Jesus who was crucified. He is not here; for he has been raised, as he said. Come, see the place where he lay."
>
> (Matthew 28:5–6)

Did you know this Scripture passage is the basis for the most important holy day in Christianity? The Easter liturgies and the liturgies of Holy Thursday and Good Friday (together called the Triduum) are our "high holy days" because they celebrate the fulfillment of God's covenant, which restores us to eternal life. The years we spend in this world are but the tiniest beginning of our life. That's the gift of Christ's death and Resurrection. Just as it is important to read about Jesus's suffering and death, it is important to meditate on the stories of his Resurrection.

Make a commitment to read the stories of Jesus's Resurrection during the Easter season. Say a prayer of thanks for the gift of eternal life.

▶ To go deeper: Read "Easter Triduum" near John, chapter 19 in the *CYB*.

It's a Good Life

Put to death, therefore, whatever in you is earthly: fornication, impurity, passion, evil desire, and greed (which is idolatry).

(Colossians 3:5)

The message here is not to hate the world or hate this life. Quite the opposite, this world is a creation of God, and Jesus entered completely into his life on earth. We are to live a joyful life following Christian values. However, Christian values sometimes conflict with the values of this world, such as the desire for money and things. Setting our mind on the things above means caring for other people more than we care about the latest music, the best wardrobe, or the most popular friends. It means trying to live the Beatitudes that Jesus gave us as our guidelines for life.

Dear Jesus, help me to live a good life by valuing the things that you taught us are important.

▸ To go deeper: Read "A Top-Shelf Life" near Colossians 3:1–4 in the *CYB*.

But I Thought I Was Free

> "But God raised him up, having freed him from death, because it was impossible for him to be held in its power."
>
> (Acts of the Apostles 2:24)

Saint Peter is talking about Christ in this quotation. But he could be talking about you, too. God will free you from death because as a believer in Jesus Christ, it is impossible for you to be held in death's power. As people who have the promise of ultimate freedom, we should beware of being held captive to lesser things. Some people allow money or material things to have power over them. For some it might be another person who holds them in his or her power; for others it might be the desire to succeed or be accepted. Think about who or what holds power over you. In what ways are you free, and in what ways are you not free?

God of freedom, I want to be free of powers that are unworthy of me as a Christian. Help me open my eyes to anything that takes away my true freedom.

▸ To go deeper: Read all of Peter's first public speech in Acts 2:14–36.

God-Given Talents

"Then the one who had received the
five talents came forward, bringing
five more talents, saying, 'Master, you
handed over to me five talents; see, I
have made five more talents.'"

(Matthew 25:20)

This line from the parable of the talents reminds us of
what God wants of us. Each servant was given a certain
amount of money to invest. (A talent is more than fifteen
years' wages!) We, too, have been entrusted with certain
talents to use during our lifetime. These gifts of ours are
worth even more than fifteen years' wages. But sometimes
we feel jealous of another person's talents, rather than
recognizing and developing the talents we've been given.
How are you doing with recognizing and developing your
God-given talents?

*Holy Spirit, you bless us with gifts and talents to be used for God's
Kingdom. Help me to focus on my own gifts and how I can use them
to make God's Kingdom grow and multiply.*

▶ To go deeper: Read "The Principle of *Kuumba*" near
Matthew 25:14–30 in the *CYB*.

I See the Lord

> Mary Magdalene went and announced to the disciples, "I have seen the Lord."
>
> (John 20:18)

Mary Magdalene encountered the Lord on Easter Sunday at the tomb. Yet at first she didn't recognize him. Like Mary, it can be hard for us to recognize Christ when we encounter him. We believe that Jesus is truly present in each of us—in the strangers on the street, in our neighbors, even in our younger brothers and sisters. But like Mary Magdalene, we need eyes of faith to recognize Christ in one another. And other people need eyes of faith to recognize Christ in us, too.

Lord Jesus Christ, you came to Mary Magdalene by the tomb. I know you come to me in the people I live with, work with, and go to school with. Give me eyes of faith so that I can recognize you in others today.

▸ To go deeper: Read "Resurrection Stories, Resurrection Hope" near Luke 24:1–12 in the *CYB*.

The Truth Is Freeing

Then Jesus said to the Jews who had
believed in him, "If you continue in
my word, you are truly my disciples;
and you will know the truth, and the
truth will make you free."

(John 8:31–32)

It is not always easy to know what is true. Sometimes
people say what they want us to believe rather than what
they know is true. It is even harder, at times, to *tell* the
truth. Jesus says two important things about that. The first
is that if we stay close to him and his word, it is easier to
live a life of truth. The second is that a person who tells
the truth, even when it is difficult, will be free. You will be
free from hurting others, free from wondering if your lie
will be found out, free in your heart because you have
nothing to hide.

*God of freedom, keep me close to Jesus, your Divine Word, so that I
will be truly and completely free.*

▶ To go deeper: Read "The Holy Spirit Guides Us into All
Truth!" near John, chapter 14 in the *CYB*.

Promise

> "This is my covenant with you. . . .
> I have made you the ancestor of a
> multitude of nations. . . . I will be
> their God."
>
> (Genesis 17:4–8)

God promised Abraham that Abraham would be the father of many nations, and that he would be their God. The story of Abraham and Sarah—who lived about 1,800 years before Christ—is a remarkable story of faith. Abraham had no children. He and Sarah were well past their childbearing years when God made the covenant with Abraham. Abraham believed God, and he and Sarah had a son, Isaac. God was revealing himself as a personal God, a caring God. From your own experience, describe how God is a caring God for you.

God of kept promises, help me have the same trust in you that Abraham and Sarah had so long ago. Let me not be afraid to step into the unknown when I hear you call.

▶ To go deeper: Read "Covenant" near Genesis 17:1–27 in the *CYB*.

It's a Great Day!

For great is the LORD, and greatly to
be praised;
he is to be revered above all gods.
(Psalm 96:4)

Some days we become very aware of God's presence
and we want to praise God. Maybe your team was the
underdog in an athletic competition and beat the previous
champions; maybe you had a successful food drive and
supplied groceries to needy families; maybe you had the
courage to stand up against the evils of racism and
discrimination and defend someone from prejudice. We
are the hands and heart of Jesus Christ on earth today.
Follow the psalmist's example and remember to praise
God for the good you do in his name.

*Dear Jesus, give me the desire to be your hands and heart in the
world. May I be compassionate and courageous in helping the needy
and confronting evildoers.*

▸ To go deeper: Read "Admit It!" near Jeremiah 22:18–23 in
the *CYB.*

The Right Priorities

> They devoted themselves to the apostles' teaching and fellowship, to the breaking of bread and the prayers. . . . All who believed were together and had all things in common.
>
> (Acts of the Apostles 2:42–44)

The early Church had the right priorities. Its members were enthusiastic for all that Jesus Christ had meant to them. The Apostles taught as Jesus had taught them. They helped all in need. They pooled their resources so that everyone would have enough food and clothing. They prayed and celebrated the Eucharist. Sometimes we look back with envy on those glorious days and wonder why our lives have gotten so complicated. Why do we spend so much time making sure we have the right clothes? being popular? playing more video games? It is a worthwhile meditation to see how our priorities match those of the first Christians.

Holy Spirit, you inspired and enabled the disciples of Christ two thousand years ago to set the right priorities. Be with us as we set our priorities and live them out today.

▶ To go deeper: Read "Christian Community" near Acts 2:43–47 in the *CYB*.

Saying Yes to God

"Here am I, the servant of the Lord;
let it be with me according to your
word."

(Luke 1:38)

Mary had the courage to respond positively when she was asked to be the mother of Jesus. This faithfulness to God's request posed many difficulties for Mary. She was engaged to Joseph, but not yet married. She must have wondered what her parents would think. What would the neighbors say? How would she explain this mysterious pregnancy to Joseph? During those trying times, she trusted God to be her strength. Because of Mary's courage and strength, God was able to send us his Son, Jesus. When we say yes to God, we can change the world.

God our creator, give me the courage to faithfully respond to you in my life, as Mary did in hers. I ask this in the name of Jesus and through the power of the Holy Spirit.

▶ To go deeper: Read "Mary of Nazareth" near Luke 1:26–46 in the *CYB.*

Being Responsible

If you choose, you can keep the
commandments,
and to act faithfully is a matter of
your own choice.

(Sirach 15:15)

Every day we make choices. Some are small ones, such as
what to wear or what music to listen to. Others are more
important. They may even affect other people, such as
how we drive or how we talk about someone. Some
choices may affect us for a long time, such as how
seriously we study for school. We don't always choose
wisely, but Sirach reminds us that we do have a choice.
Sirach didn't want the people of his time to avoid taking
responsibility by blaming their poor choices on other
people or events.

*Thank you, God, for giving me freedom in my life. With each
passing year, I have more decisions and more freedom. Help me to
choose what is right and to be responsible for the choices I make.*

▶ To go deeper: Read "Taking Responsibility" near Sirach
15:11–20 in the *CYB*.

The Call

The LORD called me before I was
        born,
    while I was in my mother's womb
        he named me.

(Isaiah 49:1)

Naming someone means you have a close relationship to
the person. Parents name children. Pet owners name dogs
and cats. God goes a step further with Isaiah. Isaiah was
going through some tough times. He felt a sense of
failure. God cheers up Isaiah by reminding him that God
named him even before he was born. God reviews the
mission he has given Isaiah and the bonds he has with
him. That's how involved God was in Isaiah's life. God
knew each of us, too, before we were born; he gave us a
mission and witnessed our naming at our baptism. Isaiah's
mission was to be a light to the nations. What is your
mission?

*Carefully consider what you think your God-given mission is in life.
Do a service or action for someone else that comes out of your
mission.*

▸ To go deeper: Read "Called to Be Prophets!" near Daniel,
    chapter 14 in the *CYB*.

Betrayal

> "What will you give me if I betray him to you?" They paid him thirty pieces of silver. And from that moment he began to look for an opportunity to betray him.
>
> (Matthew 26:15–16)

Jesus knew the pain of being betrayed by one of his closest friends and disciples. To be betrayed by a friend is one of the most devastating experiences one can have. When our trust in someone is broken, we feel angry and hurt. We can betray friends, too, even unintentionally. It might not be for money, but it could be for personal comfort. For example, we may pull away from a friend who is going through a personal loss because we find it too depressing or difficult to deal with. Your betrayal might not result in the death of a friend, but it would certainly result in pain for your friend.

Dear Lord, enable me to be a faithful friend and to support my friends, especially when they feel isolated.

▶ To go deeper: Read "Jesus' Imperfect Friends" near Matthew 26:36–45 in the *CYB*.

Take Refuge in the Lord

I sought the LORD, and he answered
me,
and delivered me from all my fears.
(Psalm 34:4)

Life can be scary. We are afraid of making the wrong decisions about what courses to take, where we should go to college, what to do for a career. We wonder if we will ever fall in love, if we will be good parents, if we will have friends. We struggle with preparing for tests and worry about not doing well on them. We may not be happy with our relationship with our parents. Our boss takes advantage of us. The psalmist had those same worries, and found that when he shared his plights with the Lord, God calmed his fears. God invites us to share our thoughts and feelings of fear with him.

Loving God, enable me to share my private thoughts and fears with you, knowing that you will be with me and give me the assurances I need.

▶ To go deeper: Read and meditate on Psalm 34.

Do Not Be Afraid

"It is I; do not be afraid." Then they wanted to take him into the boat, and immediately the boat reached the land toward which they were going.

(John 6:20–21)

The Apostles were out at sea, and a storm came up. They were terrified when they saw Jesus walking on the water. He calmed them and gave them a sense of security. Sometimes we find ourselves feeling trapped. It could be a self-made trap or something that just happened to us. We feel isolated and afraid. We think we have no one to turn to. The good news is the calming influence that is available to us is the same calming influence the disciples had. Jesus, through the power of the Holy Spirit, is with us. We are not alone. We do not need to be afraid. We can turn to Jesus to calm our fears.

Jesus, you gave us your Spirit to calm our fears and to be with us in our struggles. Nudge me to call on the Holy Spirit in times of trouble and fear.

▶ To go deeper: Read "Do You Trust Jesus?" near Matthew 14:22–33 in the *CYB*.

People, the Highlight of God's Creation

Then God said, "Let us make humankind in our image, according to our likeness; and let them have dominion over the fish . . . the birds . . . the cattle . . . all the wild animals . . . every creeping thing."
(Genesis 1:26)

The fact that God created the world and all of us to care for it is at the heart of our Christian faith. The dignity of all people is based on the reality that we are each created in the image and likeness of God. That is the basis for respect, care, and concern for one another. But the Creation story also tells us that we are called to use the resources of the earth wisely. We are God's caretakers of all the air, water, and natural life around us. We need the plant and animal world in order to survive. We need to care for it so that the generations who come after us may have a healthy world in which to live.

Name five action steps you can take to help the world's natural resources survive unpolluted. Find several friends who will work with you on those things.

▶ To go deeper: Read "In the Beginning" near Genesis, chapter 1 in the *CYB*.

Forget the Small Stuff

> So if you have been raised with Christ,
> seek the things that are above, where
> Christ is, seated at the right hand of
> God. Set your minds on things that
> are above, not on things that are on
> earth."
>
> (Colossians 3:1–2)

The Resurrection of Christ helps us to be optimists about
life. Being baptized into this mystery give us hope that
even when things seem dismal, there is light at the end of
the tunnel. Because we know that Christ has conquered
death and brought us new life, we don't have to "sweat
the small stuff." And our Christian hope allows us to take
the high road in our relationships. We can give people the
benefit of the doubt. We can more easily forgive the faults
and sins of ourselves and others. When we seek the things
that are above, we can embrace the important things in
life and let the unimportant things go.

*Lord, Jesus Christ, you conquered death by your life of faithfulness
to God. Enable me to put my energies into the significant things in
life through the power of the Holy Spirit.*

▶ To go deeper: Read Colossians 3:1–17.

Visions and Dreams

> "'I will pour out my Spirit . . .
>   and your sons and your daughters
>   shall prophesy,
> and your young men shall see visions,
>   and your old men shall dream
>   dreams.'"
>
> (Acts of the Apostles 2:17)

How do we see the future? As dark and dismal? full of terrorism and war? Or full of possibility—a future where justice and hope prevail? Proverbs 29:18 says, "Where there is no vision, the people get out of hand" (New Jerusalem Bible). We need to tap into the positive energies embedded in the Gospel message to create an optimistic vision for the future. Once we have the vision, we can devote our energies to making it happen. Without a positive vision, we dissipate our energies and stand little chance of making a significant difference.

Come, Holy Spirit, inspire me to articulate a vision that will rally my energies and help me create a more just and hopeful world.

▸ To go deeper: Read "Vision Quest" near Joel 2:28–29 in the *CYB.*

Singing God's Praise

Make a joyful noise to God, all the
earth;
sing the glory of his name;
give to him glorious praise.

(Psalm 66:1–2)

The psalmist has good days and bad days, like most of us.
Today is a day when things are going well and he wants to
praise God. Think of the ten best things that have
happened to you in your life. How was God involved in
those things? Who else was involved? Think of ways you
can praise and thank God with the same enthusiasm as
the psalmist. How can you thank the other people who
contributed to the good things in your life?

*Compose your own way of thanking God and singing his praises. Be
as passionate as the psalmist.*

▸ To go deeper: Read and pray all of Psalm 66.

Abundant Mercy

> Let us therefore approach the throne of grace with boldness, so that we may receive mercy and find grace to help in time of need.
>
> (Hebrews 4:16)

Some days are awesome and others are dismal. Our faith tells us that we can approach God for love and mercy on all days. You may find it is easier to thank God and praise him than to beg him for help and mercy. However, we need to be bold and ask God for support in dealing with our concerns and troubles and the injustices we have endured. Because Jesus died for us, was raised by the Father, and sent us the Holy Spirit, we have abundant resources at our disposal. We are the losers if we lack courage and do not approach God for his grace and the energy to get through hard times.

Dear Jesus, you poured out your love for me on the cross. Empower me through your Holy Spirit to ask for mercy and grace in my times of need.

▶ To go deeper: Read "Approach God Boldly!" near Hebrews 4:14–16 in the *CYB*.

Breaking Bread

> When he was at the table with them,
> he took bread, blessed and broke it,
> and gave it to them. Then their eyes
> were opened, and they recognized
> him.
>
> (Luke 24:30–31)

This is the part of the Emmaus story where the two
disciples did not recognize the resurrected Jesus as he
walked with them, but they did recognize him when he
later shared a meal with them. Meals are opportunities for
us to gather, share food, and share our lives. Whether we
are having fast food or a family birthday meal, we have an
opportunity to listen to others and hear their stories.
Especially in the Gospel of Luke, many of the significant
things Jesus did were in the context of a meal. How can
we make our meals real times of sharing and affirming
one another? How can we recognize Christ in one another
at our meals?

*Participate in a meal where you are deliberately conscious of sharing
stories, listening, and affirming others. Where was Christ at the
meal?*

▸ To go deeper: Read "Jesus Is with Us!" near Luke 24:13–35
  in the *CYB*.

Sticking It Out

"Do you also wish to go away?"
Simon Peter answered him, "Lord, to
whom can we go? You have the words
of eternal life. We have come to
believe and know that you are the
Holy One of God."

(John 6:67–69)

The Apostles were tempted to abandon Jesus and his teachings. Some of their friends did. But as Peter acknowledged, they had no one else to turn to because they had come to believe and know that Jesus was sent from God. We, too, are tempted to ignore Jesus and his teachings. We sometimes feel his teachings are too hard, too complicated, not much fun, and curtailing our freedom. But through God's grace, we are nudged back to embrace the Gospel of Christ as the best way to live our lives with meaning and purpose. We are encouraged by the Christian community to "stick it out" for happiness here and hereafter.

Blessed Trinity, empower me to be a faith-filled disciple of Jesus Christ even when I am tempted to ignore his teachings and promises.

▶ To go deeper: Read John 6:60–71.

Good News in Action

"Go into all the world and proclaim
the good news to the whole creation."
(Mark 16:15)

The challenge is to proclaim the good news so it is perceived as good news by those who hear it. In a nutshell, the good news of the Gospel, as proclaimed in the life, death, and Resurrection of Jesus Christ, is that each of us is loved and cherished by God. Sometimes we proclaim the good news not with words but with actions. Sticking with a friend through hard times is one way of helping the person to know that she or he is cherished by God as well as by us. At another time our action may be remaining loyal to a friend when others turn against her or him. Proclaiming the good news is seen in words and in actions!

Reflect on the needs of your family and friends. What actions can you take to affirm them and help them feel loved and cherished? How is this related to proclaiming the good news?

▶ To go deeper: Read "Jesus Strengthens Our Faith" near Mark 16:1–20 in the *CYB*.

Ambassadors of Peace

"Peace be with you. As the Father has sent me, so I send you."

(John 20:21)

We are called not only to wish peace for others, but to be ambassadors for peace. Where do we begin? Look for the cause of violent situations. Hint: Where injustice and intolerance prevail, you will find little hope of peace. What situations in your school, community, or home need peaceful solutions? Are injustice and intolerance causing the lack of peace? If so, what can you and your friends do to bring about peaceful solutions? What is Jesus asking you to do today to bring peace into your life and the lives of those you touch?

God of peace, give me wisdom to identify the causes of conflict in my family, my community, and our world. Let me be your ambassador of peace by addressing these causes before they lead to more violence.

▸ To go deeper: Read "Becoming a Peacemaker" near Romans 12:17–19 in the *CYB*.

It's All in the Name

It was in Antioch that the disciples were first called "Christians."

(Acts of the Apostles 11:26)

We are proud to be called Christians, but we may not have thought about what that means. In the early Church, people began to identify with Christ as the teacher whom God raised from the dead. They knew Jesus as a person who lived among them, who died for them, and who was raised by God to new life. Jesus had taught that he would not leave us orphans, and that he considered the early Christians to be not only his friends but his brothers and sisters. Because of this, we can identify with him and be called Christians. Being proud to be Christian carries the responsibility to act like a Christian—like Christ.

Jesus the Christ, you have called us your disciples, your friends, and your brothers and sisters. Enable us to proudly be identified as Christians who carry on your work on earth.

▸ To go deeper: Read: "Introducing Barnabas" near Acts 11:19–26 in the *CYB*.

Living Water

"Everyone who drinks of this water will be thirsty again, but those who drink of the water that I will give them will never be thirsty. The water that I will give will become in them a spring of water gushing up to eternal life."

(John 4:13–14)

Jesus talks of giving us living water, which is the water we receive at baptism. Notice the dynamic words used to describe the living water, "a spring of water gushing up to eternal life." The living waters of baptism continue to work for us during our whole life. Being immersed in water at our baptism empowers us to deal with the many death and resurrection moments in our lives. However, sin and a lack of attention to our spiritual life can block the flow of this living water. The Easter season is a good time to nurture our relationship with God and know the joy and power that comes with Christ's living water.

God our Father, you have given us Jesus Christ, who gives us new life through baptism. Remove everything in my life that prevents me from quenching my spiritual thirst.

▸ To go deeper: Read "How Deep Is Your Well?" near John 4:1–42 in the *CYB*.

It's All Worth It!

"For God so loved the world that he gave his only Son, so that everyone who believes in him may not perish but may have eternal life."

(John 3:16)

God's great love for us is shown by his sending his Son, Jesus, to be one of us, to be our brother and our friend, to show us how to live, and to share eternal life. God knew that assuming human nature and dealing with all the situations we run into was not going to be easy. So he gave us the best he had as a role model—his Son, Jesus Christ. And the best news is that after his Ascension, Jesus is here for us 24-7, as the expression goes. Believe in Jesus and tap into the power and life he makes available to us every moment of every day.

Dear Jesus, help me to be aware of your availability and your presence as I struggle to live my life like you lived yours.

▸ To go deeper: Read "Nic at Night" near John 3:1–21 in the *CYB.*

Just Believe!

"I am the way, and the truth, and the life. No one comes to the Father except through me. If you know me, you will know my Father also."

(John 14:6–7)

God is always there for us. Christ shows us the way to the Father. So why do we worry so much? Maybe because being aware of God's presence in our lives is difficult with so many distractions. We worry about doing well in school, about making friends, about grandparents who are ill, about our families, about our jobs. We sometimes act as if we do not know we have a God who loves us and wants us to be happy. We forget that we have someone who walks with us through our entire life, someone who loves and cares for us, and someone who wants us to know that he has things under control.

Holy Trinity, you have made my life secure and meaningful. Help me to remember your presence and not to waste my energy worrying about things that are in your control.

▶ To go deeper: Read "The Way, and the Truth, and the Life" near John 14:6–7 in the *CYB*.

Sing a New Song

O sing to the LORD a new song,
  for he has done marvelous things.

(Psalm 98:1)

This time of year brings many signs of new life. What are the signs of new life in your neighborhood? Think of all the new life God provides and for which you are grateful. Now think of your favorite music. Which songs would you want to sing to God? Which songs express the goodness of the world? Imagine you are a DJ and your show is dedicated to positive music, music you could use to thank God for all the marvelous things he has done. What music would you use? Why?

Consider creating a prayer time during which you would listen to your favorite music that expresses your joy in God and his creation. You might even sing along with the music as part of your prayer.

▶ To go deeper: Read and meditate on Psalm 98.

Greater Works
Than Jesus's?

"Very truly, I tell you, the one who believes in me will also do the works that I do and, in fact, will do greater works than these, because I am going to the Father."

(John 14:12)

Jesus calls us, as believers in his message, to do what he has done—to use everything in our power to make people whole. He calls us to care for people, to feed the hungry, to visit those in prison, to clothe the naked, to serve others who are in need. What about the "greater works"? Jesus could be referring to all the things that were not even invented when he lived: the medical advances, the scientific achievements, the technical knowledge that have opened new doors and new opportunities to make people whole. We are challenged to use those greater works for the good of others and to further the Kingdom of God.

God of power and might, help me use the talents and resources of this earth to continue to build your Kingdom, so rich in the values that Jesus Christ taught us.

▸ To go deeper: Read John 14:1–14.

Saint Mark, the Evangelist

> Cast all your anxiety on him, because he cares for you. Discipline yourselves, keep alert.
>
> (1 Peter 5:7–8)

Mark was a disciple of Saint Peter. An early Church tradition says that Mark wrote the earliest Gospel, a Gospel full of little details that the author may have learned from Peter. Peter's epistle reminds us to not be anxious about the worries of the world because Christ truly cares for us. Though we are to cast our fears to the Lord, we are, at the same time, to be disciplined and alert to the pitfalls we may find in life. Being disciplined in reading the Scriptures daily and reflecting on how they apply to our lives is one way to be an alert disciple of Christ.

Christ, my redeemer, I want to follow you. Enable me to be disciplined in my prayer life and my Scripture reflection so that I may be a faithful follower.

▸ To go deeper: Read the introduction to the Gospel According to Mark in the *CYB*.

Leave Your Troubles Behind

"Peace I leave with you; my peace I give to you. I do not give to you as the world gives. Do not let your hearts be troubled, and do not let them be afraid."

(John 14:27)

Jesus gives us peace not in a superficial way, but in a way that relieves us of stress and tension. The disciples were fearful that they would feel abandoned when Jesus left them. Jesus assures them that they will have the Holy Spirit to guide them. Jesus also wants us to be at peace. If we believe that the Holy Spirit is continually with us, we need not worry about the small disappointments in life, the things that irritate us, or the things that shake our confidence. We need to leave our troubles in God's hands and focus on being peaceful and bringing peace to others.

Jesus, you are our model of peace. You bring it to wherever people are open to your message and your life. Empower me to do the same.

▶ To go deeper: Read "The Peace of Christ" near John 14:27 in the *CYB*.

Bread of Life

> "I am the bread of life. Whoever comes to me will never be hungry, and whoever believes in me will never be thirsty."
>
> (John 6:35)

Jesus tells us that he is the living bread. The symbolism of bread is rich. Bread's nutrients give us the energy we need to go about our lives. Jesus tells us that when we eat the bread of the Eucharist, we are absorbing all his values, his grace, and his energy to use in furthering the Kingdom of God. Jesus also tells us that his life will satisfy us. Our longing for meaning and purpose in life will be achieved in consuming Jesus, the bread of life.

Christ, Bread of Life, be with us, inspire us, nourish us, help us find meaning and purpose in life. Be with us so that we may never be hungry or thirsty again.

▸ To go deeper: Read "The Eucharist" near John, chapter 6 in the *CYB*.

Cut Out the Old Stuff

> "I am the true vine, and my Father is the vinegrower. He removes every branch in me that bears no fruit. Every branch that bears fruit he prunes to make it bear more fruit."
>
> (John 15:1–2)

We probably have a lot of "stuff" in our lives, and we probably do a lot of "stuff" that is not very important. God wants us to get rid of the stuff that is not helping us grow in discipleship—that may be interfering with what God really wants us to accomplish. Vinegrowers prune off dead branches and prune back the good ones so that they will bear more fruit. If we allow God to be the vinedresser in our lives, what would he cut out or cut back? What excess materials can we give away? Can we cut back on activities we spend a lot of time on but that lead us nowhere?

Dear Jesus, you told the story of the vinedresser so that we could be more effective disciples. Give me the courage to cut out those things that are not helping me grow closer to you.

▸ To go deeper: Read and pray "Not of This World" near John 15:18–25 in the *CYB*.

Saint Catherine of Siena

"Do you understand what you are reading?" He replied, "How can I, unless someone guides me?"

(Acts of the Apostles 8:30–31)

Saint Catherine of Siena was a laywoman and a mystic. When she lived, in the fourteenth century, three men claimed to be Pope, but only one was the duly elected Pope. Catherine was influential in guiding the Church to recognize the true Pope, thus avoiding a crisis. This made her unpopular with those who were supporting the false popes, and an attempt was made on her life. Sometimes we, too, are called to act with the integrity of Catherine and speak the truth, even when it is not popular. Think of circumstances in which you might be called to do that, and prepare yourself for them.

God, our creator, you gave us Catherine of Siena as a model to guide us. Strengthen us to have the courage and integrity that she had to speak the truth, even when it was not popular.

▸ To go deeper: Read "Bearing Good News" near Acts 8:26–40 in the *CYB*.

How Much Love?

"This is my commandment, that you love one another as I have loved you. No one has greater love than this, to lay down one's life for one's friends."

(John 15:12–13)

Love is one of those words that is used so casually. It is used for a piece of clothing, a car, a house, even a book. It is heard between spouses, children, family members, and friends. But Jesus gives us the benchmark for what great love really is. It is great love if it truly reflects the desire to lay down one's life for one's friends. Jesus did just that. He gave his life to show how much he believed in his Father and how much he believed in us. He trusted that we would take full advantage of what his life and death offer us and continue his mission by sharing his love with others.

Dear Jesus, you have shown us how to love. Empower us to make a difference in the world by loving others as you have loved us.

▶ To go deeper: Read "Christ Lives in Us Through the Holy Spirit!" near John, chapter 16 in the *CYB*.

Saint Joseph, the Worker

> Whatever your task, put yourselves
> into it, as done for the Lord and not
> for your masters, since you know that
> from the Lord you will receive the
> inheritance as your reward.
>
> (Colossians 3:23–24)

Saint Joseph was a carpenter. Joseph and Jesus, his helper, saw dignity in work and had a job that was of service to others while it supported their family. No matter what our work—full-time or part-time, studying or helping at home—Paul reminds us to do it for the right reason. Adolescents can feel a lot of pressure to choose their future path and to make sure it will pay well. Remember that your life's work is building up the Kingdom of God. Choose work that honors the talents God gave you, not just the work that will get you further ahead by the world's standards.

Have a conversation with an adult who knows you well and ask that person what general direction in life she or he sees your talents taking you.

▸ To go deeper: Read "The Principle of *Ujima*" near Deuteronomy 8:11–18 in the *CYB*.

Getting Along Together

But when the Jews saw the crowds, they were filled with jealousy; and blaspheming, they contradicted what was spoken by Paul.

(Acts of the Apostles 13:45)

It is sometimes said, "Where two or three are gathered, there is conflict." Whether it's a shouting match in a synagogue as in Paul's experience, conflicts in our church, arguments at home, people taking sides at school or at work, no one gets a free pass on conflict in life. Because conflict is inevitable, the important thing is to learn how to handle it in a healthy and productive way. Some schools and YMCAs sponsor conflict-management workshops for teens to learn such skills.

Come, Holy Spirit, and fill me with understanding and patience so that I can be creative at bringing peace wherever I find conflict.

▶ To go deeper: Read "Divisions in the Church" near 1 Corinthians 1:10–17 in the *CYB*.

Saint Philip, Apostle

Philip said to him, "Lord, show us the
Father, and we will be satisfied."

(John 14:8)

Jesus never said it would be easy to be a believer. Certainly
the Apostle Philip didn't find it easy. He doubted Jesus
could feed the multitude with loaves and fish. And he was
chosen by Jesus to be an Apostle! We may have our ups
and downs in our faith, but God stays with us through it
all. Perhaps Philip's secret is that he hung in there. It may
have been years before he was a firm believer, but he
never stopped giving it a chance. Right now Mass may
seem boring, the Bible may seem confusing, prayer may
seem hard, and going to church may be looked down on.
Be like Philip. Hang in there and stay close to your leader.

*Dear Jesus, Saint Philip stayed close to you even when he had his
doubts. Help me to also stay close to you, especially when my faith is
wavering and I'm unmotivated to do anything about it.*

▸ To go deeper: Read "Feed Your Soul" near 2 Kings 4:42–44
in the *CYB*.

Actions Speak
Louder Than Words

> Better to be poor and walk in integrity
> than to be crooked in one's ways
> even though rich.
>
> (Proverbs 28:6)

"With Jamie, what you see is what you get." What a wonderful compliment! Jamie is described as a person of integrity. The dictionary says integrity means being undivided or integrated. In other words, people of integrity don't say one thing and do another; they act according to what they believe. They're not one person on the inside and another on the outside. The quote from Proverbs reminds us that if you cannot keep your integrity and be successful in the world, then give up worldly success.

Holy God, Jesus had complete integrity in everything he said and did. It didn't make him wealthy or always popular, but he was a perfect success in what really mattered. Help me to do the same.

▶ To go deeper: Read "Integrity" near Proverbs 28:6 in the *CYB.*

The Ascension of the Lord

> When he had said this, as they were
> watching, he was lifted up, and a cloud
> took him out of their sight.
>
> (Acts of the Apostles 1:9)

As Jesus left this earth, he told the gathered Apostles that
they would be his witnesses to the ends of the earth. He
was talking to them and to all generations of his followers.
They and we are to take Christ's place in a real sense.
Whether we're at camp, traveling on vacation, busy with
exams, or watching television with our brothers or sisters,
we are to bear witness to others of what it means to
behave like a Christian.

*Where might you travel in the coming summer months? Write down
for yourself one thing you can say or do each morning to remind
yourself to be a Christian witness when you travel.*

▶ To go deeper: Pray "I Will Follow" near Matthew 28:16–20
  in the *CYB*.

Speak Fearlessly About Faith

One night the Lord said to Paul in a vision, "Do not be afraid, but speak and do not be silent; for I am with you."

(Acts of the Apostles 18:9–10)

People laughed at Marisa because of the way she spoke. Other kids made fun of Kevin when he talked about his faith. But both Marisa and Kevin would not let themselves be intimidated. They would not let others decide for them whether or not to speak. They would not let someone else make them silent. You haven't had a vision of the Lord speaking as to Paul. Nevertheless, the words he heard are meant for you also. When you are speaking the truth of what you believe, you can be absolutely certain that the Lord is with you just as truly as he promised to be with Saint Paul.

Saint Paul, sometimes, like you, I'm afraid to speak about my faith. I want to have your courage to speak for God and about God to others.

▶ To go deeper: Read "Help Us Evangelize" near Acts, chapter 17 in the *CYB*.

Having a Troubled Heart

"Do not let your hearts be troubled.
Believe in God, believe also in me."

(John 14:1)

Sometimes we *do* feel troubled. Things go wrong.
Someone gets seriously sick. We do poorly on an exam. A
friend turns against us. We don't get chosen for the team.
The words of Jesus's to the Apostles and to us can be
consoling in such times. No matter what happens, no
matter what we do, our God is here with us to help us.
No matter what! When we feel alone and troubled, we
just have to be still and take the time to talk over what is
in our heart.

*O God who loved me so much to give me life, be with me during
difficult times. Help me to be still and listen, to be wise and
courageous in facing what is troubling my heart.*

▶ To go deeper: Read "Randy's First Day of School" near
  Psalm 42 in the *CYB*.

Give Me a Grateful Heart

> "'I have set you to be a light for the
>   Gentiles,
>   so that you may bring salvation
>   to the ends of the earth.'"
> When the Gentiles heard this, they
> were glad and praised the word of the
> Lord.
>
> (Acts of the Apostles 13:47–48)

When the Gentiles heard from Paul and Barnabas that
Christ had died and risen and that they, too, had heaven
open to them, they were thrilled. This great good news is
something we so take for granted. Imagine people in our
day being excited and praising the Lord spontaneously
because Christ has opened heaven to us. This is worth
meditating on—do we take for granted the wonderful
news of salvation? How can you recapture the sense of
awe and wonder over all that Christ has done for us?

*Jesus, you weren't forced to come and live as one of us. You chose to
suffer and die for us as you did. I want to live with an attitude of
gratefulness for this and for all the gifts God has given me.*

▸ To go deeper: Read "A Courageous Stance" near Acts
  14:1–7 in the *CYB*.

God Doesn't Make Junk

> "And the one with the two talents also came forward, saying, 'Master, you handed over to me two talents; see, I have made two more talents.'"
>
> (Matthew 25:22)

Leanne and Carlos spent a lot of time watching other kids and comparing themselves with them. They seemed to feel that they were not as smart or popular or talented as everyone else. Sometimes they would make jokes about others because of the envy they felt. In fact, Leanne and Carlos each had gifts and abilities just waiting to be developed, if only they paid more attention to them. They were the opposite of the servant in the parable. Ask someone who knows you well to help you name your gifts and talents. Each day this week, tell someone you know what talent you think he or she has.

O God who created all things, I thank you for the abilities and talents you have given me. Help me to develop them and use them responsibly and generously.

▸ To go deeper: Read "Each New Day" near Lamentations 3:22–26 in the *CYB*.

Blessed Damien of Molokai

"And now I know that none of you, among whom I have gone about proclaiming the kingdom, will ever see my face again."

(Acts of the Apostles 20:25)

Damien was a farm boy in Belgium who had to quit school as a teenager. Eventually he became a priest and volunteered to go to a remote island in Hawaii where people with the terrible disease of leprosy were isolated. He spent his life there, contracted the disease himself, and died far away from home. Have you ever had to tell a good friend good-bye? That's what both Saint Paul and Damien had to do. Separation from a good friend, even if it is for a good reason or an important family decision, can be painful.

If you have been separated from people who are important to you, send them an e-mail or phone them to tell them what's going on and to let them know that you still care about them.

▶ To go deeper: Read and pray "Good-bye to a Friend" near Acts 20:36–38 in the *CYB*.

We All Need Friends

When they arrived, they called the church together and related all that God had done with them, and how he had opened a door of faith for the Gentiles.

(Acts of the Apostles 14:27)

Paul and Barnabas knew how important it is to have a community of friends to support you. They'd just returned from some hard times, and when they arrived, they invited the group together to share the stories of their trip. Friends and family in the faith community are like the good soil that keeps us rooted and firmly planted. Sometimes we don't have a natural group with which to share our problems and joys. If that is the case, you may have to take the initiative to make that happen. It is worth the time and energy to find a group who will give the support and positive influence you want and need.

Holy Spirit, keep me connected to a group of Christians that can support one another in being faithful followers of Jesus. Show me the people who need such support from me.

▸ To go deeper: Read "Encouragement" near 1 Thessalonians 3:6–13 in the *CYB*.

Stay Connected

"I am the vine, you are the branches. Those who abide in me and I in them bear much fruit, because apart from me you can do nothing."

(John 15:5)

"No man is an island," the saying goes. Our experiences and feelings tell us we need to be connected. Jesus says that if we are to call ourselves his followers, we need to be as firmly connected to him as branches are to the trunk. That is a good analogy because everyone knows what happens to a branch when it is cut off—it withers and dies. Jesus also declares that staying connected to him promises that we will bear much fruit, that is, we will have a life that is worthwhile, satisfying, and helpful to others.

Come, Holy Spirit, and keep me connected to Jesus. May everything I do and say and think be a reflection of my connection to Jesus so that I may bear good fruit.

▸ To go deeper: Read "Make Your Home with Jesus" near John 15:1–11 in the *CYB*.

For What Are You Hungry?

> "'Lord, when was it that we saw you hungry and gave you food, or thirsty and gave you something to drink?'"
>
> (Matthew 25:37)

"Man, I'm starving!" We hear people say this so easily, people who don't have an idea what it means to be starving. Many people are truly hungry or thirsty and have nothing to eat or drink. But people also have different kinds of hunger besides physical hunger. Some would say their loneliness is a hunger for companionship or friendship. Others would describe their hunger as a longing to know what they're supposed to do with their life. Overworked single parents are hungry for some peace and quiet and a bit of time alone. What kinds of hunger and thirst do you see around you?

Spirit of God, open my eyes and my heart to the needs of others. Help me find ways to "feed" all the different kinds of hunger that people have.

▸ To go deeper: Read "Hunger Pains" near Nehemiah, chapter 5 in the *CYB*.

Saint Matthias

For I am honored in the sight of the
LORD,
and my God has become my
strength—

(Isaiah 49:5)

For years Matthias followed Jesus. He was with him from the time John the Baptist baptized Jesus until Jesus ascended into heaven. It wasn't until after the Ascension that the Apostles selected him to replace Judas.

Melissa worked much harder on the team project than the others, but they all got the same grade for it. Raphael was passed over for the lead in the school musical because another student's father donated a piano to the school. We don't always get the recognition we might see as fair. When that happens to you, the test of your character is to keep doing what is right and to do it without resentment or bitterness.

Saint Matthias, help me to persevere as you did, knowing that my reward may or may not come in this life.

▶ To go deeper: Read Isaiah 49:1–6.

Come, Holy Spirit

"But you will receive power when the Holy Spirit has come upon you; and you will be my witnesses."

(Acts of the Apostles 1:8)

God keeps promises. God the Father, who gave us our life and the world to sustain it, promised to send the Son to redeem us. Jesus came, lived among us, died, and rose to keep that promise. Christ also promised to send the Holy Spirit to be with each of us throughout our life. He said we would not be left orphans, and we're not. The Holy Spirit is as present to you as to the Apostles on Pentecost. In the sacrament of Confirmation, we receive the gift of the Holy Spirit in a special way. With the Holy Spirit's presence in your life, you are empowered to fully live as a disciple of Jesus Christ.

Come, Holy Spirit, and shower me with your spiritual gifts so that I may live my Christian life to the fullest!

▸ To go deeper: Read "Confirmation" near Acts 2:1–13 in the *CYB*.

We All Experience Doubt

Immediately the father of the child cried out, "I believe; help my unbelief!"

(Mark 9:24)

In a world that gives highest honor to what can be scientifically proven, being a Christian is countercultural. God became man? Christ rose from the dead? It is normal to sometimes wonder and question and test our faith. In the end faith is a gift from God. We *choose* to believe or not. That doesn't mean it isn't sometimes hard to believe. Mother Teresa said she had great doubts about her faith from time to time. That's why throughout our lives, the prayer of the child's father is a good prayer to remember: "Lord, I believe; help my unbelief."

How do you respond when you have doubts about your faith or what the Church teaches? Ask the Holy Spirit for the gifts of knowledge and understanding.

▸ To go deeper: Read "I Believe; Help My Unbelief!" near Mark 9:14–29 in the *CYB*.

Do Not Suffer Alone

"Do not human beings have a hard
service on earth,
and are not their days like the days
of a laborer?"

(Job 7:1)

The story of Job is an extended reflection on why bad things happen to good people. Every time it seemed things couldn't get any worse for Job, they did. God was not punishing Job, but he was allowing Satan to test Job. Through it all Job's friends sat with him and allowed him to express his frustration.

Kids made such fun of Eric that he could hardly bear to go to school. He spent most of his time alone, and was even thinking of suicide. In confiding to his only friend, he was convinced to talk to a counselor. That may have saved his life. It is important to know that like Job, we do not have to endure suffering alone.

Jesus, you made us to help one another. Give me the strength to ask for help when I need it.

▶ To go deeper: Read "Suffering" near Job 7:1–21 in the *CYB*.

It Can Be Hard Not to Judge

And Jesus said, "Neither do I condemn you. Go your way, and from now on do not sin again."

(John 8:11)

Marietta and Tony had sex. That decision soon brought many other serious decisions for themselves, their families, and their classmates. Now she was pregnant. The gossip tree at school was soon buzzing. Reactions to the news varied. Some people giggled and laughed. Some condemned them and avoided talking with them. Others wanted to help them make the best out of a difficult situation. What do you think you'd do? Jesus gives a clear answer to a similar situation. He doesn't approve but he doesn't judge. He also expects the behavior to change. How do you think he would treat Marietta and Tony if he were a classmate?

Dear Jesus, I praise you for your compassion for others. Help me to have your attitude of not approving of someone's sinful actions but always loving the person despite her or his sin.

▶ To go deeper: Read John 8:1–11.

Do I Have Faith?

Now faith is the assurance of things
hoped for, the conviction of things
not seen.

(Hebrews 11:1)

Sometimes what we've always believed and accepted as
children can seem unbelievable as we grow older. As you
grow older, you will make decisions for yourself about
what you believe, not just follow certain beliefs because
your parents do. Julie stopped being involved in church
because she felt it didn't mean anything to her. Francis,
too, didn't feel he was getting anything out of Mass, but
kept going while he sought answers to his questions. Who
demonstrated more hope and integrity? We owe it to
ourselves to seriously study what we believe so that we
can grow into an adult faith.

*Loving God, stay with me every step of the way as I search for you
on my journey to an adult faith.*

▶ To go deeper: Read "How Do You Spell Faith?" near
Hebrews 11:1–3 in the *CYB*.

Saint Bernardino of Siena

I will most gladly spend and be spent for you.

(2 Corinthians 12:15)

Saint Bernardino was a Franciscan who was a great preacher, traveling from town to town on foot, often preaching for hours to great crowds. He was a leader of his order and established schools of theology for his monks. Even before Bernardino was a priest and preacher, he, with other young men in his hometown, offered to run the local hospital during the plague. Later he spent a year caring for a beloved aunt until she died. He was a living example of what Paul meant in the verse above. Bernardino spent time each day in prayer and reflection to stay connected with God, the source of his energy.

Resolve to spend quiet time each day just listening to the voice of God in your heart. Stay connected to God, who is the source of all spiritual energy.

▸ To go deeper: Read "When I Am Weak, Then I Am Strong!" near 2 Corinthians 12:1–10 in the *CYB.*

Like Little Children

"Let the little children come to me; do not stop them; for it is to such as these that the kingdom of God belongs."

(Mark 10:14)

There is a big difference between being childish and being childlike. Jesus was talking about the latter when he addressed his disciples. Children are born good and trusting. They are not sarcastic and cynical. Young children are eager to help and are joyous and grateful. What other qualities do you see in young children that are worth having as an adult? What can we learn from "such as these" to whom the kingdom belongs? Look into volunteering at a place where younger children are cared for. You might read stories, play ball, or help with homework. You and they would benefit!

Blessed Trinity, Father, Son, and Holy Spirit, I want to regain some of the blessed qualities I had as a child. Help me remember this today.

▶ To go deeper: Read "Teaching Others" near 2 Timothy 2:22–26 in the *CYB*.

Holy Trinity

"Go therefore and make disciples of all nations, baptizing them in the name of the Father and of the Son and of the Holy Spirit."

(Matthew 28:19)

We call the Father, Son, and Spirit the Holy Trinity. But it is impossible to understand how we can have only one God but three persons. This we believe on faith. But what a gift to have three persons in the Godhead to whom we can relate! Sometimes we pray to the Father when our heart needs connection to our divine parent. Other times it is helpful to pray to Jesus Christ, who experienced the joys and sorrows we do. The Holy Spirit is with us now in a presence of wisdom and understanding, fortitude and counsel, knowledge, piety, and respect for the Lord—all gifts of the Spirit.

Father, Son, and Holy Spirit, I thank you for your presence to me at different times. I thank you for coming to us as our father, our brother, and the Spirit who dwells within us.

▸ To go deeper: Read "Trinity Sunday" near Matthew 28:16–20 in the *CYB*.

Never Alone with God

> "The hour is coming, indeed it has come, when you will be scattered, each one to his home, and you will leave me alone. Yet I am not alone because the Father is with me."
>
> (John 16:32)

This is another example of how fully human Jesus was. He knew that he would suffer loneliness when his friends abandoned him during his suffering. He reminded them (and himself) that even without them he was not alone, because his Father was with him. That feeling of being alone is one of the most painful in human life. Who can you go to when you need someone? Ask God to help you find a good companion for times when you feel alone. Know that even when no one is around, God is with you.

Heavenly Father, I know you are always with me, but sometimes I need the physical support of other friends. Keep people close to me to remind me of your love.

▸ To go deeper: Pray "A Prayer for Friends" near John, chapter 17 in the *CYB*.

Give God the Best

> Be generous when you worship the
> Lord,
> and do not stint the first fruits of
> your hands.
>
> (Sirach 35:10)

Make a list of what God has given you. If you are honest about it and take the time to think, it will be a very long list! It will include the chance to be alive, to have the talents, friends, family, and opportunities you have, and much more. Jesus tells us over and over the importance of sharing what we have. Sirach says we should not be stingy in giving our best—"the first fruits of your hands"—back to God. Do you give the best of your talents, your time, and your finances through service and charity? That is also called being a good steward, and it is an important part of the life of a Christian.

Write down the ways in which you give the best of yourself—your talents, your time, your treasures—back to God through service and charitable giving. Are you satisfied?

▸ To go deeper: Read "Stewardship: Making a Contribution" near Luke 21:1–4 in the *CYB*.

Do Unto Others

Have mercy upon us, O God of all.
(Sirach 36:1)

For thousands of years, people have been asking God for mercy. It could be because they've neglected their relationship with God, the friend who is always there even when ignored. Sometimes mercy is needed because of a serious failing or sin. Or it may be that we ourselves have not been merciful but have judged others, criticized them publicly, or gossiped about what we see as their shortcomings. Maybe we have kept them out of our group. That is not how we would want God to treat us. This is not how God wants us to treat one another.

Holy Spirit, be with me when I am tempted to judge and criticize another.

▸ To go deeper: Read "God Cares for Those Who Suffer Persecution!" near Psalm 140 in the *CYB*.

The Gift of Nature

> I will now call to mind the works of
>   the Lord,
>   and will declare what I have seen.
> By the word of the Lord his works are
>   made;
>   and all his creatures do his will.
>
> (Sirach 42:15)

Did you ever drive into a forest or hike through an area with no houses or people for miles around? That would be a tiny taste of the wonderful world God gave us to enjoy and to keep us fed and alive. This incredible and free gift of God's creation is lent to us. There may be as many or more generations after us who need to use it as there have been between Adam and Eve and our generation. We cannot afford to waste it or ruin it. Whether we are conserving water or recycling or carpooling, we are showing gratitude to God, respect for the earth, and responsibility for generations to come.

Creator God, I thank you for the gift of nature and the many ways it feeds and sustains us. I pledge to do all that I can to preserve and care for this gift for future generations.

▶ To go deeper: Read "The Beauty of Creation" near Philippians 4:8–9 in the *CYB*.

Saint Augustine of Canterbury

"Keep up your courage! For just as you have testified for me in Jerusalem, so you must bear witness also in Rome."

(Acts of the Apostles 23:11)

Saint Paul heard these words from Christ when he was being physically threatened for speaking about his faith. Centuries later the Pope sent Saint Augustine of Canterbury and forty other monks to England to preach about their faith. Many of the monks were so frightened that they wanted to return home right after they got there. It is not easy to talk about your faith or to stand up for it. Someone asks for your help to cheat on a test or a term paper. Someone ridicules your habit of attending Sunday Mass. Someone wants you to help him or her get a false I.D. Don't make a U-turn. Keep up your courage!

Saint Augustine of Canterbury, my fears may not be of dying in a strange country, but I can easily lose my courage, too. Be with me when I need to defend my faith.

▸ To go deeper: Read "Sharing Your Story" near Acts 22:6–16 in the *CYB*.

If You Love Me . . .

> [Jesus] said to him the third time, "Simon son of John, do you love me?" . . . And [Peter] said to him, "Lord, you know everything; you know that I love you." Jesus said to him, "Feed my sheep."
>
> (John 21:17)

We love different people in different ways. The love between a married couple or the love parents have for their children is different than the love we have for friends. We also mean something quite different when we say we love all people. And then there is our love for God. Jesus connects our love for God with taking care of others. He tells Peter that *if* Peter loves him . . . *because* Peter loves him, Peter will feed his sheep. In other words Jesus says that if you love me, take care of those I love. And that includes everyone.

Dear Jesus, yes, I love you, and like Peter I will express that love by caring for those you care for—everyone, everywhere.

▸ To go deeper: Read "The Humble Church" near John 21:15–19 in the *CYB*.

How to Be Well Fed

> The cup of blessing that we bless, is it not a sharing in the blood of Christ? The bread that we break, is it not a sharing in the body of Christ? Because there is one bread, we who are many are one body, for we all partake of the one bread.
>
> (1 Corinthians 10:16–17)

Catholic Christians believe that in the Eucharist, the Mass, the wine is changed into the blood of Christ and the bread into the body of Christ. This mystery is at the heart of our faith. When we celebrate this sacrament, we are connected with believers from centuries past, with believers today all over the world, and especially with the community with whom we are worshiping. We are fed spiritually to help us live the way we are called to live as followers of Christ. We hear the Scriptures and are fed. We receive Christ's body and blood and are fed. This food changes us and makes us strong.

Resolve to attend Mass this weekend. Really listen to what you hear and what you pray in the prayers. Allow yourself to believe that you are fed in the Eucharist.

▶ To go deeper: Read "The Eucharist" near Luke 22:14–23 in the *CYB*.

A Temptation for Our Time

So do not be foolish, but understand
what the will of the Lord is. Do not
get drunk with wine, for that is
debauchery; but be filled with the
Spirit.

(Ephesians 5:17–18)

To fit in with the crowd, to not be looked down on, to
feel good, to escape from feeling bad—these and many
other reasons are given by adolescents to explain why they
drink alcohol. Teens that resist the temptation to drink
accomplish those same things in ways that do not risk
harm to themselves or others. Staying in control, being
content enough with myself, respecting my body, caring
too much for my friends to take chances—these are some
reasons teens give for not drinking. What would you add
to the list?

*Loving Creator, my body is a temple for the Holy Spirit. I don't
want to abuse it any more than I would abuse our church. I need
you to help me resist the pressure to abuse alcohol.*

▸ To go deeper: Read "Alcohol" near Ephesians 5:10–20 in the
  CYB.

The Visitation

> In those days Mary set out and went with haste to a Judean town in the hill country, where she entered the house of Zechariah and greeted Elizabeth.
>
> (Luke 1:39–40)

Mary was given the greatest privilege of any human being. If anyone ever had reason to be proud and egotistic, it was she who was asked to be the mother of the Son of God. Instead she has two remarkable reactions that demonstrate her humility. First she forgets about herself and travels to another town to help care for her cousin Elizabeth, who is expecting a baby (John the Baptist). The account of their meeting is powerful. The unborn infant John jumps with joy in the womb. Then Mary prays the beautiful prayer called the Magnificat, in which she proclaims God's goodness rather than taking any credit herself.

Pray to Mary to help you follow her example in caring for others and being a person of humility and gratitude.

▶ To go deeper: Read the story of Mary's visit in Luke 1:39–56.

So What Am I to Do?

Make me to know your ways, O
      LORD;
   teach me your paths.
Lead me in your truth, and teach me,
      for you are the God of my salvation;
      for you I wait all day long.
                              (Psalm 25:4–5)

If I only knew what God wanted of me, I'd do it. But how do I know? Most of us don't wake up with a note from God on our dresser. When we were children, God spoke to us through our parents or other caring adults. We knew we had a loving God because most of us experienced loving adults in our lives. As a young adult, you must now begin to take responsibility for your own prayer life and relationship with God. You will find that God speaks to you through other people, through the events in your life, through the Scriptures, and through your prayer and reflection. All those things will shape your vision of how you can make a difference in the world.

O Lord, I long for you to show me the truth of who I am and who you call me to be. Let me be more aware of your presence, and teach me your ways through the people and events in my life.

▶ To go deeper: Read and pray "Integrity and Values" near Psalm 26 in the *CYB*.

Love God
and Love Your Neighbor

> "'You shall love the Lord your God with all your heart, and with all your soul, and with all your mind, and with all your strength.' The second is this, 'You shall love your neighbor as yourself.'"
>
> (Mark 12:30–31)

Loving God with our whole selves is difficult. What were the signs of love that Jesus recognized? Through his stories and teaching, we learn that we love God if we are honest, if we are generous, if we don't brag about our abilities, if we identify with the poor, if we are compassionate, if we are peacemakers, and if we are respectful of our parents and teachers. Loving our neighbor is easier to comprehend, but then Jesus throws in the challenge—do we love our neighbor as much as we love ourselves? What things do you do to show you have a healthy love of self? How is that related to loving your neighbor?

List all the things you do to show you have a healthy love of self. Pray to Jesus to show you how to love your neighbor as yourself.

▶ To go deeper: Read and pray "What Do You Want from Me?" near Mark 12:13–17 in the *CYB*.

Sacred Heart of Jesus

"Come to me, all you that are weary and are carrying heavy burdens, and I will give you rest."

(Matthew 11:28)

We tend to get overwhelmed with worries at times: You wonder how well you will do on finals. Will you get a summer job? Will your friends want to do things with you in the summer? Will you have to baby-sit your younger brother or sister? Today is the feast day of the Sacred Heart of Jesus—when we celebrate how big and loving Jesus's heart is. The Gospel reading for today reminds us that Jesus wants us to bring our worries to him, to unburden ourselves. He tells us that we are making life too complicated by worrying about unimportant things. If we worry less and focus on his love for us, we will be happier.

Sacred Heart of Jesus, I implore you to help me simplify my life, worry less, and be concerned about what is really important in life—living for the good of others.

▸ To go deeper: Read "God's Love" near 1 Corinthians, chapter 13 in the *CYB*.

Suffering Is Part of Life

"Now you have observed my teaching, my conduct, my aim in life, my faith, my patience, my love, my steadfastness, my persecutions, and my suffering. . . . What persecutions I endured! Yet the Lord rescued me from all of them."

(2 Timothy 3:10–11)

Reflect on how a person might describe your life by observing your conduct, your apparent goals, your faith, and how you handle suffering. Where have you been patient, loving, and steadfast? Note how sufferings were an intimate part of Saint Paul's life. How have you been able to deal with suffering, especially if you perceive it to be unfair? Sometimes even friends and family cause incredible suffering. Sometimes the suffering is so intense that one questions the value of living. Following Saint Paul's example, turning our suffering over to Jesus lessens the burden and leads to hope.

Dear Jesus, strengthen me when and if my suffering seems too intense and unfair. Help me to share the burden with you and decrease my pain.

▶ To go deeper: Pray "For Those Who Walk with Us" near 2 Timothy 3:12–14 in the *CYB*.

Be Sober

As for you, always be sober, endure suffering, do the work of an evangelist, carry out your ministry fully.

(2 Timothy 4:5)

The work of the evangelist is to spread the Good News. What is the good news you need to spread at this time in your life? Is the proclamation to avoid underage drinking one that needs to be heard by your friends and classmates? If the temptation to drink alcohol is widespread, what things can you do to help others see the many problems associated with drinking? Teenage sexual activity, depression, theft, and violence are often connected to alcohol. This is an area where you have an opportunity to accomplish a great mission—to stop underage drinking.

Holy Spirit, give me the courage to speak out against teenage drinking and to inspire other teens to live soberly.

▸ To go deeper: Read "Misleading Messages" near 2 Timothy 4:1–5 in the *CYB*.

Clues to Happiness

"Blessed are the poor in spirit. . . .
Blessed are those who mourn. . . .
Blessed are the meek. . . .
Blessed are those who hunger and
thirst for righteousness. . . .
Blessed are the merciful. . . .
Blessed are the pure in heart. . . .
Blessed are the peacemakers."

(Matthew 5:3–9)

People were often pressing Jesus for the answer to living
holy and happy lives. Did it take anything more than
following the commandments? In the Sermon on the
Mount (Matthew) and the Sermon on the Plain (Luke),
Jesus lays out his answers at the beginning of his public
life. In these sermons he begins with the Beatitudes,
which are highlighted above. Read the complete Scripture
passage and decide what actions you can take to live the
Beatitudes. What does it mean for you to be poor in
spirit? mourning? meek? merciful? a peacemaker?
Develop an action plan to carry out your insights.

*Dear Jesus, you taught the disciples what they needed to do to be
happy and obtain eternal life. Assist me as I ponder the Beatitudes
and find ways to live them in my life today.*

▸ To go deeper: Read "An Upside-Down Kingdom" near
  Matthew 5:1–12 in the *CYB*.

Let Your Light Shine

"You are the light of the world. A city built on a hill cannot be hid. No one after lighting a lamp puts it under the bushel basket, but on the lampstand, and it gives light to all in the house."

(Matthew 5:14–15)

Often we lack the confidence in our own skills and relationships to really let our light shine. We tend to hide behind the cloak of false modesty and keep our gifts covered up. Jesus tells us that we are the light of the world. That means we need to take the risk of exploring our gifts and using them for the good of others. Hiding them is denying what God has done for us, what God has given to us. Think of one or two talents you have, and develop a plan for how you can use them for the good of others—thus letting your light shine so other people's lives will be better.

Lord God, you gave me talents and gifts to be used to create a better world. Help me to explore those gifts and use them for the good of others.

▸ To go deeper: Read Matthew 5:13–16.

Generosity Brings About Miracles

"Make me a little cake . . . and bring it to me, and afterwards make something for yourself and your son."

(1 Kings 17:13)

This passage is from a story about Elijah asking a widow to make a simple meal for him. She told him she had to use the last of her grain and oil to make food for her and her son. Elijah asked the widow to fix his food first. She did and had enough food left for her household for many days. When we serve others and don't worry about ourselves, God also provides for us. We save for the latest designer clothes or the newest technology or sports equipment without thinking that people are going to bed in cardboard boxes. How can we put our needs in perspective and focus on the needs of others?

Lord God, you gave us this wonderful story of the widow's generosity, which was rewarded by a miracle. Help me to be generous and not count the cost as I try to imitate her trust.

▸ To go deeper: Read "Introducing Elijah and Elisha" near 1 Kings, chapter 17 in the *CYB*.

Reconciliation Is Key

"If you remember that your brother or sister has something against you, leave your gift there before the altar and go; first be reconciled to your brother or sister, and then come and offer your gift."

(Matthew 5:23–24)

God does not want us to be hypocrites. And it would be hypocritical to worship the God of love and forgiveness while we have broken relationships with family members or friends that we haven't tried to reconcile. Jesus calls us to work toward reconciliation with anyone who has a grievance against us. We need to be willing to ask for forgiveness and to extend forgiveness. Recall some relationships you have that are stressed or tense. What is the cause of the tension? What can you do to bring about reconciliation?

Dear Jesus, you gave up your life for the forgiveness of sin. Enable me to seek forgiveness from those I have offended and to give forgiveness to those who have offended me.

▶ To go deeper: Read and pray "A Lord's Prayer Reflection" near Matthew 6:5–15 in the *CYB*.

Are You a Clay Jar?

> But we have this treasure in clay jars,
> so that it may be clear that this
> extraordinary power belongs to God
> and does not come from us.
>
> (2 Corinthians 4:7)

People will only know about Jesus if we make him visible by our actions and words. But we do not need to be perfect; in fact, we cannot be perfect. That is good, though, because if people thought the good we do comes easily, they wouldn't understand that God is our strength and that God alone is the one we must turn to. When we speak out even though our words are clumsy, when we serve the elderly even though it means sacrificing some free time, when we act with forgiveness even though are hearts are filled with anger, then we are the clay jars that Saint Paul talks about.

Holy Spirit, I know I am not always eager to be a disciple. Let my effort to act in Jesus's name, even when it isn't easy, be a witness to others about your power in my life.

▶ To go deeper: Pray "Fill Me, Lord" near Galatians 5:22–26 in the *CYB*.

Be Direct!

"Let your word be 'Yes, Yes' or 'No, No'; anything more than this comes from the evil one."

(Matthew 5:37)

The context of this quote is Jesus's teaching on taking oaths. He is trying to caution people against wavering in their commitments, or promising one thing while intending to do another. Jesus's message is to be unambiguous in telling the truth and living your commitments. Say what you mean. Mean what you say. Sometimes people avoid telling the truth because they are afraid of the consequences. What advice do you have for those people? Why is it sometimes hard for you to tell the truth?

Dear Jesus, give me the courage to speak the truth even when I am afraid of what will happen. Strengthen me to never be part of "cover-ups."

▸ To go deeper: Read "Nothing But the Truth" near Proverbs 10:18–21 in the *CYB*.

What Are
You Called to Do?

"The harvest is plentiful, but the laborers are few; therefore ask the Lord of the harvest to send out laborers into his harvest."

(Matthew 9:37–38)

Each of us is called in some way to contribute to the building up of the Kingdom, or Reign, of God. What talents do you have? How can they be used to make God's presence felt in the world? Do you have the talents to be an engineer? a teacher? a priest? a vowed religious? a police officer? a newscaster? a journalist? a parent? a nurse? No matter what your talents may be, they are needed to further the mission of Christ on earth!

Blessed Trinity, Father, Son, and Holy Spirit, give me the insight to realize how my talents can be used for your greater glory and the strength to use them in that way.

▶ To go deeper: Read Matthew 9:35—10:15.

Miracles Happen When People Share

> And taking the five loaves and the two fish, he looked up to heaven, and blessed and broke them, and gave them to the disciples to set before the crowd. And all ate and were filled.
>
> (Luke 9:16–17)

Jesus had been working all day, and crowds were still following him. The Apostles wanted everyone to go home, but Jesus said no, they needed to be fed. The dilemma was how to feed thousands of people with five loaves and two fish. It was the generosity of one person that started the ball rolling. From such a gracious offering, Jesus could bless what was shared and there was enough for all to eat. Think of ways you can share what you have, and encourage your friends to share so that God can bless what you have to make a significant difference in the lives of others.

Jesus, you always had great expectations of the goodness of people. Support me as I encourage my friends to share their possessions so that others may benefit in a significant way.

▶ To go deeper: Read "Mission Possible" near Luke 9:1–6 in the *CYB*.

My Rock

In you, O LORD, I seek refuge;
  do not let me ever be put to shame;
  in your righteousness deliver me.
Incline your ear to me;
  rescue me speedily.
Be a rock of refuge for me,
  a strong fortress to save me.

(Psalm 31:1–2)

Rocks and fortresses are symbols of strength. People search for them at times of turmoil and disillusionment. When we are disillusioned by friends, family, the government, society, to whom can we turn? The psalmist cries out to God to be his rock, his fortress, his strength. God will hear us and save us from the disappointments of life. How can you identify with the psalmist's idea of God as a fortress, a rock? Under what circumstances would you call out to God as a stronghold, a fortress?

Lord God, be my rock and fortress through the ups and downs in

life. I need your protecting strength to survive as a beloved disciple of Jesus, the Christ.

▶ To go deeper: Read "How Do You Image God?" near

Wisdom of Solomon, chapter 7 in the *CYB*.

Generosity Is a Plus!

God loves a cheerful giver. And God
is able to provide you with every
blessing in abundance, so that by
always having enough of everything,
you may share abundantly in every
good work.

(2 Corinthians 9:7–8)

No one likes to receive a gift from someone who gives it
grudgingly. We feel like saying "keep it" when it is given
with a negative attitude. Saint Paul reminds us that the
more generous we are, the more abundantly God will
bless us. Many people have less than you do. You don't
have to wait until you are an adult to respond to their
needs. What kind of things can you share? Can your
sharing help change a system that is producing poverty?

*Do some research on the causes of poverty. Make a plan with others
from your church or school to take steps to address one or more of
these causes. Pray to the Holy Spirit as you do this.*

▶ To go deeper: Read "Christians Share Their Money Out of
  Solidarity!" near 2 Corinthians, chapter 8 in the *CYB*.

Praise God

Praise the LORD!
I will give thanks to the LORD with my
whole heart,
in the company of the upright, in
the congregation.

(Psalm 111:1)

God has done great things for us. One athlete was
bemoaning the fact that he had broken his leg and was
out for the season. He was feeling sorry for himself until
one of his classmates was diagnosed with inoperable
cancer. Yet the young man with cancer could still express
gratitude to God for the short life he had experienced. He
could do this because, like the psalmist, he was looking at
the bigger picture. Name things for which you wish to
praise God. How do you praise God with your whole
heart? When you look at the bigger picture, with what
great things has God blessed you?

*In your own words, thank God with your whole heart for the great
things he has done for you.*

▸ To go deeper: Read and reflect on Psalm 111.

Don't Be Fooled

"Beware of false prophets, who come to you in sheep's clothing but inwardly are ravenous wolves."

(Matthew 7:15)

Today we are always in danger of being fooled by advertising, by media stars, by popular movies, and by countless other influences. They are the false prophets of our time. They try to get us to buy their message—a message of how to stay ahead, how to get even, how to spend our leisure time. But their values are not the ones found in the Gospel. Their message is not about taking care of creation, loving your neighbor, or honoring God. Look for three ads or songs that do not reflect Gospel values and three that do. How do you respond to each of them?

Holy Spirit, help me to look beyond what is superficial in the media, discern the values by which I want to live, and do something to root out the evil of materialism found in our society.

▶ To go deeper: Read "Media Literacy" near Proverbs 1:10 in the *CYB*.

Choose Between God and Money!

"No one can serve two masters. . . . You cannot serve God and wealth."

(Matthew 6:24)

Does this verse mean that wealthy people cannot love God and be disciples? No, it means that you cannot devote your life energies to making money without caring about the impact it has on other people, the earth's resources, and especially your relationship with God. Choosing wealth over Gospel values is always a temptation. You may be tempted to take a job that interferes with your studies, so you have more spending money. Some people are tempted to do illegal things, like sell drugs, to make lots of money. Where do you experience such temptations?

Dear Jesus, you pointed out the temptation concerning wealth. Help me to recognize this temptation in my life and strengthen me to make the right decisions.

▶ To go deeper: Read "Money Talks" near 2 Chronicles 9:13–28 in the *CYB*.

Parents Worry

> "Child, why have you treated us like this? Look, your father and I have been searching for you in great anxiety."
>
> (Luke 2:48)

When Jesus and Mary could not find Jesus, they were worried. Your parents have many of the same fears. They worry when you don't come home at the agreed-upon time, when you are not with the people you say you will be with, when they smell alcohol on your breath, when your grades slip, when you hang out with the "wrong crowd." They worry when you take the car and are driving around with your friends. You can't solve all your parents' worries, but good communication with them and a plan for emergencies will alleviate some of their fears. Have a conversation with them about their concerns.

Holy Spirit, help me to be responsible about my actions and to communicate well and regularly with my parents.

▶ To go deeper: Read "The Holy Family" near Luke 2:41–52 in the *CYB*.

Who Are We?

In Jesus Christ you are all children of
God through faith. As many of you as
were baptized into Christ have clothed
yourselves with Christ.

(Galatians 3:26–27)

Our clothes often identify us. We choose to wear our
school colors, the logos of our favorite professional
teams, shirts with the name of our favorite bands. We are
proud to be identified with these people or groups. But
what does it mean to be clothed in Christ? Being clothed
in Christ is a metaphor that means our beliefs and actions
reflect the attitudes, beliefs, and values of Jesus. The way
we speak and live shows we are proud to be identified
with him. When people see you, how are they reminded
of Christ?

*Holy Trinity, I wish to clothe myself with the values and attitudes of
Christ. Enable me to become more like Christ in my words and
deeds in order to be worthy of the name Christian.*

▶ To go deeper: Read "Radical Equality" near Galatians 3:28 in
the *CYB*.

The Golden Rule

"In everything do to others as you would have them do to you."

(Matthew 7:12)

The Golden Rule is a good reminder of how we should treat others. But how many times does this rule get bent every day? Someone treats us badly, and we become vengeful and want to get even. We ignore those with whom we have little in common rather than make the effort to make a connection. Younger siblings irritate us, and we just want them to go away. We have a personality clash or get competitive with another person. Or our best friend is just being cranky. Think of three people who deserve to be treated better by you. Make a conscious effort to be kind to them.

Dear Jesus, you gave us an example of how to treat others. Through your Spirit, enable me to reach out to others, even those with whom I don't easily relate, to be a sign of your presence.

▶ To go deeper: Read "The Gospel Call to Conversion" near Matthew 7:21–27 in the *CYB*.

Good and Bad

> "'Every good tree bears good fruit,
> but the bad tree bears bad fruit. . . .
> Thus you will know them by their
> fruits.'"
>
> (Matthew 7:17–20)

The Gospels are full of symbolic language. Here Jesus is
reminding us that we will be recognized by our good
works. We are good people. We try to do good things for
others. When we do, we reflect the presence of the Lord
today. Think of every day as having limitless possibilities
for doing good works for others. You can help a sibling
pack a lunch, help a friend with homework, call a grandparent without reason, send a card to someone who needs
encouragement. Reflect on the possibilities you have for
doing some good work today, showing that you are
bearing good fruit.

*Jesus, you gave us the powerful image of a strong tree producing good
fruit as a way of motivating us to be strong and to do good works.
Strengthen me to take on the challenge.*

▸ To go deeper: Read Matthew 7:15–27.

Don't Say, "I'm Only a Teenager!"

"Do not say, 'I am only a boy';
for you shall go to all to whom I send
you,
and you shall speak whatever I
command you.
Do not be afraid of them,
for I am with you."

(Jeremiah 1:7–8)

God was asking Jeremiah to take on some challenges that Jeremiah did not think he could handle because he was only a teen. God assured him that he could accomplish what God wanted and that he should not be afraid because God would be with him. Sometimes we feel like Jeremiah. Overwhelming expectations are put on us. We are expected in many ways to act like adults, but we are treated like children. What do you think God is calling you to do today? How are you relying on him to get the job done through you?

Lord God, you gave many challenges to Jeremiah and you supported him through all his trials. Support me as I discern what you are asking me to do for your Kingdom.

▸ To go deeper: Read "Who, Me?" near Jeremiah 1:4–10 in the *CYB*.

Nativity of John the Baptist

> Now the time came for Elizabeth to give birth, and she bore a son. Her neighbors and relatives heard that the Lord had shown his great mercy to her, and they rejoiced with her.
>
> (Luke 1:57–58)

John the Baptist was Jesus's cousin, and his mission in life was to prepare people for the ministry of Jesus. John was a wonderful preacher and had a great following of people. He preached repentance and baptized many people in the Jordan River. Despite his fame he never lost sight of the fact that his role was to prepare people for the coming of the Messiah. When John recognized Jesus as the Messiah, he sent his followers to become Jesus's disciples. Who are people who call you to turn your heart toward God? Who helps you recognize Jesus?

Saint John the Baptist, help me to recognize Jesus in my daily life. I pray that the Holy Spirit will help me respond to the presence of Christ wherever I find him.

▶ To go deeper: Read "The Benedictus" near Luke 1:46–80 in the *CYB*.

A Faith Journey

> Jesus said, "Go; let it be done for you according to your faith." And the servant was healed in that hour.
>
> (Matthew 8:13)

Jesus's cure of the centurion's servant is a story of faith and humility. The soldier acknowledged his unworthiness, but he believed Jesus could cure his servant. Jesus was particularly impressed with the solder's faith because the soldier was a Roman, not a Jew. Because of his faith, the soldier's servant was healed. Today, too, when we have faith in Jesus, miracles can happen. Our faith in Christ can foster spiritual, emotional, and even physical healing for ourselves and for others. We are made whole so we can continue to share God's love with the world.

Who do you know who needs spiritual, emotional, or physical healing? In faith ask Jesus to bring his healing into that person's life.

▶ To go deeper: Read "Lord, I Am Not Worthy" near Matthew 8:8 in the *CYB*.

What's My Reward?

"Whoever gives even a cup of cold water to one of these little ones in the name of a disciple—truly I tell you, none of these will lose their reward."
(Matthew 10:42)

Jesus is trying to help his disciples see that reaching out to others and serving them, even in simple things, is what is really important. To be a disciple means to do the "little things" well—to see what would make others happy and then do it. Volunteering to cut a neighbor's grass while they are on vacation or when they are sick is the work of the disciple. Surprising your family by baking a dessert is another example of sharing your talents with others. Name simple things you will do for others this summer. What's your reward? Knowing the joy of sharing Jesus's love.

Dear Jesus, strengthen me to look for simple ways to serve others in your name and thus truly live like your disciple.

▶ To go deeper: Read "Divine Humility, Cosmic Glory" near Philippians 2:1–11 in the *CYB*.

Rough Times

> Someone said to [Jesus], "I will follow
> you wherever you go." And Jesus said
> to him, . . . "The Son of Man has
> nowhere to lay his head."
>
> (Luke 9:57–58)

As Jesus traveled to Jerusalem, where he would ultimately
be killed, some of his disciples made promises of commitment to him. Jesus challenged their commitment because
he wanted them to know that rough times were ahead.
Jesus was looking for disciples who were committed to
following him through good times and hard times. To
follow Jesus includes being with him on the good days,
when everyone is pleased with you, and on the bad days,
when people are plotting against you. When do you find it
easy to follow Jesus? When is it hard?

*Spirit of God, be with me when I am tempted to slack off in
following Jesus. Empower me to be a faithful disciple in hard times
as well as good times.*

▸ To go deeper: Read "Jesus' Temptations, My Temptations"
  near Matthew 4:1–11 in the *CYB*.

Saint Irenaeus

> "No one after lighting a lamp puts it
> in a cellar, but on the lampstand so
> that those who enter may see the light.
> . . . If then your whole body is full
> of light, with no part of it in darkness,
> it will be as full of light as when a
> lamp gives you light with its rays."
>
> (Luke 11:33–36)

Saint Irenaeus was a bishop and a martyr. One of his insights was that the glory of God is found in a person who is fully alive. His positive attitude toward the potential for human development in relationship to God set an upbeat tone for his ministry. He encouraged people to be the best they could be because that gives glory to God. Despite his optimistic view of people, he suffered like the Israelites who wandered in the desert for forty years before being led into the Promised Land. From Irenaeus we learn that we let God's light shine through us by embracing everything that life offers us, sometimes even the inevitable suffering.

God of life, help me to be fully alive by embracing all the experiences, all the people, and all the joys and sorrows that life offers me. Let me not reject anything you send to help me become more fully human.

▸ To go deeper: Read "Prayer That Does Justice" near Amos 5:21–24 in the *CYB*.

Saints Peter and Paul

I have fought the good fight, I have
finished the race, I have kept the faith.
(2 Timothy 4:7)

Saint Peter and Saint Paul were early leaders in the
Church. Peter was the Apostle recognized by Jesus as his
leader. Paul never met Jesus. In fact, he even persecuted
Jesus's disciples before he experienced conversion to the
person and mission of Jesus. After that time Paul spent his
whole life spreading the good news that Jesus was Lord
and Savior. Peter and Paul did not always agree on
everything, but they respected each other and were able to
work out their differences. They both kept their faith in
Jesus despite imprisonments and hardships. They truly
fought the good fight and finished the race.

*Dear Jesus, your saints give us wonderful examples of faith-filled
discipleship despite many hardships. Help me to learn from Peter
and Paul how to be an effective leader today.*

▸ To go deeper: Read 2 Timothy 3:10—4:8.

Value of Human Life

And Abraham looked up and saw a ram, caught in the thicket by its horns. Abraham went and took the ram and offered it up as a burnt offering instead of his son.

(Genesis 22:13)

This story about Abraham and Isaac emphasizes Abraham's complete trust in God. But it also has an important pro-life message. During Abraham's time some people practiced child sacrifice because they thought it pleased their gods. That may be the reason behind Abraham's willingness to sacrifice his firstborn son. God was pleased with Abraham's faith, but stopped Abraham from killing Isaac because God values human life and does not desire human sacrifice. We must continue to carry that insight through today, calling our society to respect all human life from conception to natural death.

Do some research about all aspects of the Respect Life movement. Decide on action steps you will take to respect all human life.

▸ To go deeper: Read "Ultimate Trust in God!" near Genesis 22:1–19 in the *CYB*.

Miracles All Around Us

He then said to the paralytic—"Stand up, take your bed and go to your home." And he stood up and went to his home.

(Matthew 9:6–7)

When we listen to the miracle stories, we are amazed. You might be surprised to know that in Jesus's time, he wasn't the only miracle worker around, and people expected the miracle to teach something or reveal something about the miracle worker. Even though you don't work miracles of curing people, your actions reveal a lot about you, too. Think about the things you said and did during the past week. Which ones are you proud of? What do these say about you? Perhaps they say that you were unselfish or thoughtful or humorous or that you had courage.

Pay attention in the coming days when you see someone work a "miracle" by acting generously, helpfully, or courageously. Mention to the person that you admire what he or she did.

▶ To go deeper: Pray "Spiritual Paralysis" near Matthew 9:1–8 in the *CYB*.

You Are Called

As Jesus was walking along, he saw a man called Matthew sitting at the tax booth; and he said to him, "Follow me." And he got up and followed him.

(Matthew 9:9)

Joanna knew since she was seven years old that she wanted to be a doctor when she grew up. Greg had helped in the family hardware store for as long as he could remember, but didn't see it as his future. Some people seem so certain about what path in life they will take. Other people may feel as though they will never figure it out. One thing we can all be sure of is this: that just as surely as Jesus called Matthew to follow him, he calls each of us. Pay attention to the things that attract you, seem interesting, and give you energy. Talk with adults who know you to get their ideas of what path you might think about following.

Come, Holy Spirit, open my eyes and heart to the work I am called to do as a follower of Jesus. Let me not be fearful but openly searching.

▸ To go deeper: Read Matthew 9:9–13.

Saint Thomas, Apostle

"Unless I see the mark of the nails in
his hands, and put my finger in the
mark of the nails and my hand in his
side, I will not believe."

(John 20:25)

This remark has caused Thomas to be remembered as
Doubting Thomas. This is the same Apostle who, when
he thought Jesus would be killed if he returned to Judea,
wanted to go with Jesus to be killed alongside him (see
John 11:16). That sounds like two different people. It
might be said that all of us sometimes act like different
people. We may have times when we act like we have
never heard the Gospel message, when we doubt that the
things we have been taught are right and true. We also
have times when we live up to our ideals and do the right
thing without question. Remember those times, and take
courage. Remember Thomas, and take heart.

*Saint Thomas, I am sometimes faithful and sometimes not. I want
to grow in trusting what God has revealed to be right and true. Help
me remember your own struggles when I am weak.*

▸ To go deeper: Read John 20:24–31.

Saint Elizabeth of Portugal

As for those who will follow this
rule—peace be upon them, and mercy.
(Galatians 6:16)

Saint Elizabeth is usually pictured with a dove or an olive
branch in her hand, both symbols of peace. Elizabeth was
the daughter of the king of Aragon. As a young person,
she learned self-discipline and acquired a taste for
spirituality. Those qualities served her well during her
adult years when she became a peacemaker in her family
and among the royal leaders of her day. She brought about
peace between her son and her husband; between the king
and his cousin who claimed the crown; and between her
son, when he became the king of Portugal, and his son-in-
law, the king of Castile.

*Dear Jesus, show me where I can be a peacemaker: at home, between
friends, in my job. Help me to follow the example of Saint
Elizabeth in helping other people overcome conflict and differences.*

▸ To go deeper: Read: "'If You Want Peace, Work for Justice'"
near Isaiah 58:6–14 in the *CYB*.

A Taker or a Giver?

> Then he said to his disciples, "The harvest is plentiful, but the laborers are few; therefore ask the Lord of the harvest to send out laborers into his harvest."
>
> (Matthew 9:37–38)

Are you a taker or a giver? It seems that so much advertising focuses on making our life easier, as if we have some divine right not to have to work hard. Yet Jesus told his disciples that God needs people willing to labor, that is, to give of themselves to bring the good news of Christ to others. Jesus is praying that people like you would be willing to be givers. The example of Jesus and the Apostles is of people who were willing to give everything for others. The irony is that it is only in giving of ourselves—our time, our energy, and our love—that we receive what is truly important in life: love and purpose.

Loving God, help me respond to Jesus's prayer by becoming a laborer for your Kingdom. Let me overcome the messages that say others should serve me, rather than that I should serve others.

▶ To go deeper: Read "A Little Gift Goes a Long Way" near John 6:1–14 in the *CYB*.

Respectful Language

Do not accustom your mouth to
coarse, foul language,
for it involves sinful speech.

(Sirach 23:13)

Swearing and using foul language wasn't invented by your generation. In the Old Testament, two hundred years before Christ, the wise man Ben Sira was advising against it. People seem to use foul language for a variety of reasons: to fit in with others, to get attention, because it's a habit, and even to annoy adults. For sure, there are other, better ways to accomplish those goals! Choosing to avoid foul language is more respectful of God, of yourself, and of those who hear you.

Challenge yourself to avoid swearing and foul language. Ask God to help you have the courage to ask others not to use it around you.

▶ To go deeper: Read "Four-Letter Words" near Sirach 23:12–15 in the *CYB*.

Where Will I See Christ?

Sow for yourselves righteousness;
  reap steadfast love;
  break up your fallow ground;
for it is time to seek the LORD.

(Hosea 10:12)

The dictionary tells us that righteousness means acting in a way that follows a divine or moral law. Jesus calls us to do more than act legalistically. He showed us that following God's law means loving God above everything else and loving our neighbor as ourselves. That is why we try to see the Lord in our neighbors, our friends, our brothers and sisters, people we don't especially like, even people we don't know but read about or hear about in the news. When we are able to do this, we will be living righteously. We will be treating others as Jesus did and as he wants us to.

Open my eyes to you, Lord. Help me see you in everyone I meet today. I know this is a challenge for me. I know I can do it with your help. Send your Spirit to help me.

▶ To go deeper: Pray "Live the Belief" near 1 Peter 1:13–25 in the *CYB*.

You Love Me So Much

When Israel was a child, I loved him,

. . . .

It was I who taught Ephraim to walk,
   I took them up in my arms.

(Hosea 11:1–3)

Imagine a toddler struggling to take a few first steps into Mother's arms. Imagine a little child running across the grass to Daddy's open arms. The prophet Hosea compares God's love to that of warm and caring parent. Like the parent in these pictures, God loves you no matter what. God's love for you is unconditional and fuller than that of anyone else who will ever love you. What is your reaction to such love? How do you want to live in response to such love?

Dear Jesus, help me see my parents with different eyes. They are people with disappointments and dreams, people who get tired and discouraged, and they love me as best they can.

▶ To go deeper: Read "Ravens and Vultures" near Proverbs 30:17 in the *CYB*.

You've Offended Me!

> Realizing that their father was dead,
> Joseph's brothers said, "What if
> Joseph still bears a grudge against us
> and pays us back in full for all the
> wrong that we did to him?"
>
> (Genesis 50:15)

Joseph's siblings had reason to worry about how he would treat them. After all, they had planned to kill him and had sold him as a slave to some passing traders. Hopefully any conflicts you have had with siblings pale in comparison! Most brothers and sisters have trouble getting along from time to time. When that happens it can be tempting to hold on to a grudge and try to get even. What an example Joseph gives! When his brothers realize later that he's in charge of the family's future and they apologize, Joseph weeps and forgives them immediately.

Reach out to a brother or a sister in some way today. Be the one to take the first step to improve the atmosphere if it is bad. If you have no siblings, mend your relationship with someone outside the family.

▶ To go deeper: Read "Sibling Rivalry" near Genesis 25:19–34 in the *CYB*.

God's Word Will Be Done

So shall my word be that goes out
    from my mouth;
  it shall not return to me empty,
but it shall accomplish that which I
    purpose,
  and succeed in the thing for which I
    sent it.

(Isaiah 55:11)

Sometimes it seems that the good we try to do doesn't bear any fruit. Your effort to be reconciled with someone is rejected. The Habitat for Humanity home you help build doesn't begin to provide for all the homeless. Your attempt to share your values or beliefs is ridiculed. But God promises in Isaiah and other places that his word, that is, his ultimate purposes will always be accomplished. This includes all our efforts to make a difference. Remember that we just see the short term and not the long haul. Take comfort in knowing that God is in charge.

God of fulfilled promises, let me remember that you are in charge and that I don't need to be concerned when my efforts to do your will sometimes seem to be unsuccessful.

▶ To go deeper: Read Isaiah 55:6–13.

Saint Benedict

> "Whoever welcomes you welcomes me, and whoever welcomes me welcomes the one who sent me. . . . Whoever gives even a cup of cold water to one of these little ones in the name of a disciple—truly I tell you, none of these will lose their reward."
>
> (Matthew 10:40–42)

Be hospitable. Jesus says that when we show a welcoming spirit, even in something as simple as giving a cup of water, we are welcoming Jesus and his heavenly father. Saint Benedict, who founded the Benedictine monasteries, lived by this verse. He stressed that the monks should show hospitality, especially to their neighbors. The Benedictines' devotion to the Eucharist is the source of their spirit of hospitality. At the Eucharist we are fed with the Scriptures and the body and blood of Christ, which strengthens us to reach out to others.

Dear Jesus, let your body and blood in the Eucharist remind me of how much I am to love others and make them feel at home in my company.

▶ To go deeper: Pray the "Mass Prayer" near Mark 14:22–25 in the *CYB*.

Be Strong

> "As I was with Moses, so I will be with you; I will not fail you or forsake you. Be strong and courageous."
>
> (Joshua 1:5–6)

As a teenager and young adult, you face many important decisions. Some of them need to be made over and over. To drink or not to drink, to stay out later than you're supposed to, to take drugs or have sex—these temptations don't happen just once. It takes courage to do what is right. It's easier to do the right thing if you have others with you. Whether your friends support you or not, you still are not alone. The Lord says the same words to you as to Joshua.

If you've been in a situation where it was hard to do the right thing, think about what helped you. If you regret your decision, talk with someone you trust to help plan what you can do the next time.

▶ To go deeper: Read "Be Not Afraid" near Joshua 1:5–9 in the *CYB*.

Seize the Day

Rejoice, young man, while you are young, and let your heart cheer you in the days of your youth.

(Ecclesiastes 11:9)

At this age life feels like an endless road stretching on and on. Taking time for granted is the easiest and most natural thing to do. Because so many thousands of days seem to stretch ahead of them, many young people do not reflect on *this* day, this gift of time. Each and every day is a gift to be "opened" and treasured. In the day-to-day busyness of school and job and sports and friends, it is up to you to stop and look at the gift and decide how to spend it. Take time to appreciate the good things that surround you and the energy and enthusiasm that come with being young.

Loving God, you are the endless gift giver! Thank you for this day. I will try to spend it with Jesus Christ at my side and the Holy Spirit leading me.

▶ To go deeper: Read "*Carpe Diem*—'Seize the Day'!" near Ecclesiastes 11:7–10 in the *CYB*.

Too Much Violence

They shall beat their swords into
    plowshares,
        and their spears into pruning hooks.
            (Isaiah 2:4)

Nearly fifty years ago, Pope Paul VI went to the United Nations and said: "No more war! War never again!" Yet wars continue to go on and on: military wars between nations, violence in our towns and cities, wars of words between people. It seems we almost get used to it and think of it as normal. But it doesn't have to be this way. In Colorado a little boy was given a free toy army tank when his mother bought him a hamburger in a fast-food restaurant, and he had no idea what it was. Imagine a world in which that is true of everyone!

Start a peace awareness campaign. E-mail your local radio and television stations and encourage them to feature stories of people working for peace.

▶ To go deeper: Read "Swords into Plowshares" near Isaiah 2:1–5 in the *CYB*.

If You Have a Problem

"Take my yoke upon you, and learn from me; for I am gentle and humble in heart, and you will find rest for your souls. For my yoke is easy, and my burden is light."

(Matthew 11:29–30)

Some people imagine that teenagers have no worries and live a carefree life. Although at times that is true, at other times life's problems are exactly the kind of heavy burden Jesus describes here. You may have situations to face, people to deal with, decisions to make, conflicts to handle, and expectations that are overbearing. Take them all to the one who is not only ready but eager to give you rest. God is the understanding father, the wise mother, the sympathetic friend you are looking for.

Find a quiet place where you can be alone for fifteen minutes. Write down the worries and problems you carry. Then talk them over with the Lord.

▶ To go deeper: Read Matthew 11:25–29.

Failure Hurts

But I said, "I have labored in vain,
  I have spent my strength for
    nothing and vanity;
yet surely my cause is with the LORD,
  and my reward with my God."

(Isaiah 49:4)

Maybe it was the test you thought you'd prepared so well for but did poorly on. Maybe it was the person with whom you tried so hard to be friends but who ended up rejecting you. Maybe it was the way you lost your temper after you had promised yourself you'd keep cool. It happens to everyone, feeling like you failed. Sometimes it is a small incident; sometimes it's something major. But even tiny failures seem big. Isaiah felt failure, yet he still expresses his trust in God. Can you do the same? What is the lesson God has for you in a failure you experienced?

Come, Holy Spirit, and help me open my eyes to see the good in what feels bad. Even Isaiah told you about feeling like this. Your promises uplifted that servant long ago. Do the same with this servant.

▸ To go deeper: Read and pray "The Servant's Success" near Isaiah 49:1–6 in the *CYB.*

Repentance

> You have taught your people
> that the righteous must be kind,
> and you have filled your children with
> good hope,
> because you give repentance for sins.
> (Wisdom of Solomon 12:19)

Since the beginning of the human race, people have done things they should not have done, things that were harmful to others and to themselves. But as redeemed and baptized people, we admit our sin, do what we can to make amends, and try harder to overcome our failure in the future. It is what is expected of us, and it is a rewarding experience. We are fortunate to have the sacrament of Penance and Reconciliation for this purpose. It is a chance to seek God's loving forgiveness and commit to overcoming the temptation of sin. This sacrament is a wonderful gift we have been given.

Find out when an opportunity will be available for you to celebrate the sacrament of Penance and Reconciliation, and put it on your calendar under "Important Things to Do!"

▶ To go deeper: Read "Reconciliation" near John 20:21–23 in the *CYB.*

Who Is Your God?

> It is he whom we proclaim, warning everyone and teaching everyone in all wisdom, so that we may present everyone mature in Christ. For this I toil and struggle with all the energy that he powerfully inspires within me.
>
> (Colossians 1:28–29)

Saint Paul was so fired up about God that he hurried from place to place preaching the good news. And when he couldn't be with a particular community in person, he wrote them letters about Christ's teachings. Because of his experience with Christ on the road to Damascus (see Acts 9:1–19), Paul was sure of who God was. Each of us has our own image of God based on what we have been taught and what we have experienced. How would you draw a picture of God? Would it be the same picture you would have drawn when you were five or ten years old? Has your idea of God matured as you have?

Jesus Christ, you are the visible image of the invisible God. Help me to grow in my understanding of God by knowing you better through God's word.

▶ To go deeper: Read "The Image of God" near Colossians 1:15–20 in the *CYB*.

Justice, Kindness, Humility

He has told you, O mortal, what is
     good;
   and what does the LORD require of
      you
 but to do justice, and to love kindness,
   and to walk humbly with your God?
                              (Micah 6:8)

The prophet Micah makes it sound so simple. In one
sentence he says what God requires. Maybe Micah can see
so clearly because he came from a simple background.
The three virtues he names are needed very much today.
There is much injustice to which we can pay attention.
There is more than enough unkindness to go around. And
examples of being humble are rarely seen on our screens
or in our papers. Choose one of these to focus on for a
few days. Look for positive examples of each virtue.
Think about ways you can put Micah 6:8 into practice.

*Come, Holy Spirit, and inspire me to live the virtues of justice,
kindness, and humility. Help me see opportunities today to live out
those virtues.*

▶ To go deeper: Read "From Humble Beginnings" near Micah
  5:2–5 in the *CYB*.

Rich Soil

"Other seeds fell on good soil and brought forth grain, some a hundred-fold, some sixty, some thirty. Let anyone with ears listen!"

(Matthew 13:8–9)

Jesus is talking to the crowd gathered around him. He is talking about you as well. You are the good soil in which the word of God has been placed. You have the ability to bring forth so much goodness over the course of your life. That goodness will grow through the vocation you live and the particular work you do. It will grow through the way you stay close to the Lord. It will grow through the way you care about others, especially those who have greater needs than you do.

Dear Jesus, while you were on this earth, you gave us so much guidance. I will try to be the good soil for your word during these years as a teen and into my adult life. Help me to think of that each day.

▸ To go deeper: Read the parable of the sower in Matthew 13:1–10.

You're One of a Kind

"Before I formed you in the womb I
  knew you,
and before you were born I
  consecrated you.

. . . .

Do not say, 'I am only a boy';
for you shall go to all to whom I send
  you."

(Jeremiah 1:5–7)

Every human being is thought of in this way by God. Every single person is so loved by the God who made her or him. Here God is telling Jeremiah—and you—that you are being sent. Furthermore, no excuses are allowed. You may feel too young, you may not feel experienced enough, or you may not feel confident. None of that matters. God has still chosen you as a messenger. Since before you were born, God knew you, loved you, and had hopes and expectations of you. You get to decide how you will live them out.

Ask your parents to tell you about the day you were born. Ask them to describe the day you were baptized. Thank God for these two loving events.

▸ To go deeper: Read Jeremiah 1:4–8.

Saint Mary Magdalene

> Jesus said to her, "Mary!" She turned and said to him in Hebrew, "Rabbouni!" (which means Teacher). Jesus said to her, ". . . go to my brothers."
> (John 20:16–17)

Despite the traditional assumption that Mary Magdalene was the sinner who anointed the feet of Jesus, that is not true. Rather, she was a woman whom Jesus freed from evil spirits (Luke 8:2), and later was a leader among the women disciples. She was one of the few who stood by the cross as Jesus died. Significantly, in John's Gospel Mary was the person Jesus appeared to after the Resurrection. Mary Magdalene may have been misunderstood for generations but Jesus chose her to be the first to share the exciting news of Jesus's Resurrection from the dead.

Saint Mary Magdalene, give me strength and confidence when I am misunderstood. I want to be neither vengeful nor self-pitying. Be with me at those times.

▸ To go deeper: Read "Introducing Mary Magdalene" near John 20:1–18 in the *CYB*.

Find a Shepherd,
Be a Shepherd

I will give you shepherds after my own heart, who will feed you with knowledge and understanding.

(Jeremiah 3:15)

We usually think of food as something we put in our mouth. This verse mentions the food of knowledge and understanding. We receive the food of knowledge and understanding through many different people. Some are teachers in the classroom and some are not. Some are older and some are our age. Who are the "shepherds" in your life who are feeding you richly with knowledge but also with understanding and an example of how to live a good life? Take advantage of the time you have with them to be fed as well as possible.

Dear Jesus, you are the great shepherd, but you place many other people in that role in our lives. Help me to learn and grow from the knowledge and wisdom of parents, teachers, priests, and peers.

▸ To go deeper: Read "Christian Leadership" near Titus 1:5–9 in the *CYB*.

The Lesson

> We know that all things work together
> for good for those who love God,
> who are called according to his
> purpose.
>
> (Romans 8:28)

Some days it really doesn't seem like all things are working together. Sometimes things just seem to go wrong or don't work out as we thought they would. Can you recall a time when something that seemed bad happened to you but later you saw the good in it? We are often blinded by the disappointment or anger we feel at the moment. Taking time to reflect later can help us see the good in an experience that at the time seemed negative. We can keep our hope alive by looking for God's hidden presence when it doesn't seem like "all things work together for good."

Journal about a specific time when you experienced some kind of difficulty or disappointment. Then write about what you can learn from the experience. Thank the Holy Spirit for the insight you gained.

▸ To go deeper: Read "Hope" near Romans 8:18–30 in the *CYB*.

Gifts Galore

> When you were buried with him in
> baptism, you were also raised with him
> through faith in the power of God.
> . . . And when you were dead in
> trespasses, . . . God made you alive
> together with him, when he forgave us
> all our trespasses.
>
> (Colossians 2:12–13)

In this one brief passage, Saint Paul speaks about two
great gifts we've been given: the gift of baptism, by which
we are raised to new life with Christ, and the gift of the
forgiveness of all our sins. Baptism, along with Confirmation and the Eucharist, brings us into the family of the
Christian faithful. With the other members of the Body of
Christ, we support one another in following Jesus Christ.
Knowing that we were dead in sin but are now alive
through God's forgiveness gives us hope and courage to
proclaim Christ to the world.

*Thank you, God, for giving me the treasure of baptism. Help me to
be unafraid to turn to you when I need forgiveness.*

▶ To go deeper: Read "Baptism" near Matthew 3:13–17 in the
CYB.

Saints Joachim and Anne

"Do not be afraid, Mary, for you have found favor with God."

(Luke 1:30)

These are the words the angel spoke to Mary when she discovered she was to be the mother of the Messiah. According to an ancient Church tradition, Joachim and Anne are the names of Mary's parents. While we do not know much about them, we do know they raised Mary to practice her faith and to be a strong and courageous person and a devoted mother. They were also Jesus's grandparents, so in a sense, this feast day is "Grandparents' Day." We would, of course, not be here if it were not for our own grandparents. Whether they live near us or far away, here on earth or in heaven, you can remember them in a special way today.

Thank you, God, for giving Mary the parents you did, so that she would be the mother that Jesus needed. Thank you for my grandparents, too. Keep them in your care.

▸ To go deeper: Read "Celebrating Families" near Sirach 3:1–16 in the *CYB*.

Your Earthly Tent

For we know that if the earthly tent
we live in is destroyed, we have a
building from God, a house not made
with hands, eternal in the heavens.

(2 Corinthians 5:1)

The earthly "tent" that Saint Paul is talking about is our
body. He also calls our body a temple of the Holy Spirit,
who dwells in each one of us. That makes it as holy as a
church building. Yet many teens and even children see
their bodies as burdens. We wish our bodies were taller or
shorter or thinner or more muscular. Even elementary
school children, especially girls, talk about having plastic
surgery. Obsessing about our body type or trying to
change it in an unhealthy way is abusing our tent, our
temple of the Holy Spirit.

*Holy Spirit, help me to be secure in my outward appearance.
Remind me that it is more important to respect my body through
exercise and nutrition than to try to change it artificially.*

▶ To go deeper: Read "It's What's Inside That Counts" near
2 Corinthians 5:1–5 in the *CYB*.

A Servant Like Jesus

"Whoever wishes to be first among you must be your slave; just as the Son of Man came not to be served but to serve."

(Matthew 20:27–28)

Jesus was a servant leader. He washed the feet of his friends after their dusty walk in sandals. He patiently listened to the arguing of the disciples, and he consoled people who were grieving. He cooked fish for his friends after their long night of fishing. He showed us how to be of service to others in quiet, human, unassuming ways. It is easy to serve someone to whom we are close, someone we like, and especially someone we want to impress. Serving without being noticed or acknowledged is the real test!

Sign up at school, at church, or with an organization to take part in a service project. Afterward spend time thinking or talking about what you learned from it.

▶ To go deeper: Pray the "Prayer of a Servant Leader" near Luke 22: 24–27 in the *CYB*.

Be Quiet! Listen!

"Martha, Martha, you are worried and distracted by many things; there is need of only one thing."

(Luke 10:41–42)

Mary was sitting quietly listening and talking with Jesus while her sister, Martha, was "distracted by her many tasks" (Luke 10:40). Your own life is so busy with so many tasks: school, family responsibilities, friends, sports, work. It's easy to understand Martha and be like her. Yet we wouldn't imagine not sitting and listening to Jesus if he came to our house. But he does! He is with you just as truly as he was present in the story of these two sisters. In the words of the Scriptures and in your heart, Jesus is with you always.

Dear Jesus, help me take time today to put aside my distractions and sit quietly like Mary and listen . . . and talk with you.

▶ To go deeper: Pray "Too Busy to Be Still" near Luke 10:38–42 in the *CYB*.

Be Your True Self

> He came to his hometown and began
> to teach the people in their synagogue,
> so that they were astounded and said,
> "Where did this man get this wisdom
> and these deeds of power? Is not this
> the carpenter's son?"
>
> (Matthew 13:54–55)

Jesus was being who he was, and the people were offended and thought, "Who does he think he is?" Did you ever pretend to be different than you are in order to be accepted by a group or to impress someone? Studies have shown that some teenage girls pretend not to be smart so that boys will not feel threatened and will like them better. Some people will do silly, illegal, or even dangerous things to be accepted by a gang or a fraternity. Follow Jesus's example and be true to yourself and your values, even if it means not being accepted.

In the coming days, when you are challenged not to be true to yourself, say in your mind, "Come, Holy Spirit, give me your gift of courage."

▸ To go deeper: Read Matthew 13:54–58.

Saint Ignatius of Loyola

Who will separate us from the love of
Christ? Will hardship, or distress, or
persecution, or famine, or nakedness,
or peril, or sword?

(Romans 8:35)

The answer to that question, Saint Paul writes to the
Romans, is no, nothing will separate us from Christ. Saint
Ignatius certainly lived that out in his amazing life. As a
soldier he had his leg shattered by a cannonball and spent
a year in a painful recovery, during which he read books
about the life of Christ and the saints. That started a journey of conversion. During this time he suffered from
intense guilt, was accused of being a heretic, and even was
imprisoned while his spiritual writings were examined.
Eventually he founded an order of Jesuit priests and
brothers and became of the most recognized saints in the
Catholic Church.

*Part of Saint Ignatius's famous prayer is "You have given me all
that I have, all that I am, and I surrender all to your divine will."
Say this prayer as you begin your day.*

▶ To go deeper: Pray "Absolutely Nothing!" near Romans
8:31–35 in the *CYB*.

Money, Money, Money

"Take care! Be on your guard against all kinds of greed; for one's life does not consist in the abundance of possessions."

(Luke 12:15)

It is so easy for us to measure ourselves and others by the amount of money we or they have. We dream of when we can have a good job and make lots of money so we can buy more things. We want designer clothes, hot cars, big houses, the latest computer games, and so much more. Most often we aren't even conscious of where those desires come from. The world we live in suggests they are important, and we just absorb the materialistic values of society. Jesus's words are a challenge to us to look at what truly matters. If life is not about having lots of things, what is it about?

Make a list of the things and people that are important to you. What makes them important? How can the things be used for the good of others?

▶ To go deeper: Read "The Greed Trap" near Luke 12:13–21 in the *CYB*.

Forget the Times
I've Messed Up!

Have mercy on me, O God,
    according to your steadfast love;
according to your abundant mercy
    blot out my transgressions.

(Psalm 51:1)

David, the psalmist, is asking God to let him start all over with a fresh slate. He knows he has sinned and missed the mark on many occasions. He also believes that God is willing to forgive him, to let him begin again and do better in the future. We, too, have been in David's shoes, recognizing that we have sinned and need help to start again. We can learn from David. He was not paralyzed by his sin. He had the courage to ask God to forgive him and help him be more faithful in the future.

Dear Jesus, help me to never be stuck in a pattern of sin. Jolt me to ask for forgiveness and to begin again as your faithful follower. I ask this through the power of the Holy Spirit.

▶ To go deeper: Read "A Fresh Start" near Psalm 51 in the *CYB.*

Faithfulness

> At that time, says the LORD, I will be
> the God of all the families of Israel,
> and they shall be my people.
> > I have loved you with an everlasting
> > love;
> > > therefore I have continued my
> > > faithfulness to you.
>
> (Jeremiah 31:1–3)

Our God is a God of extreme love and faithfulness. He
stuck with the Israelites through all their betrayals and
unfaithfulness. In his ultimate act of love, we are all
adopted as his people when we are baptized into the
death and Resurrection of his Son, Jesus Christ. Through
Scripture passages such as this one from Jeremiah, we
know that God loves us as his chosen people and will
always be there for us. This is the ultimate source of our
security. We know that we can trust God's love, even
when everything else seems to go wrong.

*Dear Jesus, thank you for calling us your brothers and sisters and
friends. Your care for us is what keeps me going on bad days. Help
me to know more intimately your love for me.*

▶ To go deeper: Read and pray "Rachel Weeps" near Jeremiah
  31:15–17 in the *CYB*.

Who Is Jesus?

He said to them, "But who do you say that I am?" Simon Peter answered, "You are the Messiah, the Son of the living God."

(Matthew 16:15–16)

People in Jesus's time recognized Jesus as a person of great spiritual wisdom and power. But they didn't really know his identity, so they kept guessing at who he really was. Some said he was John the Baptist, others thought he was one of the prophets, but Peter got the answer right. Peter saw that Jesus had a unique relationship with God. He called Jesus the Son of the living God. Because of the way Jesus treated people, the way he called for truthfulness, the way he let people know they were loved by God, Peter was able to identify him as the Messiah, the Savior. Who is Jesus to you?

Lord God, continually help me to understand who your Son, Jesus, is by studying the Scriptures and the Tradition of the Church. Help me to know Jesus as a personal friend, as my redeemer, and as my God.

▸ To go deeper: Read "Peter the Rock" near Matthew 16:13–20 in the *CYB*.

Promises of the Heart

> But this is the covenant that I will make with the house of Israel after those days, says the LORD: I will put my law within them, and I will write it on their hearts.
>
> (Jeremiah 31:33)

Remember how the covenant that God made with the Israelites was inscribed on stone tablets? Today we often summarize it as the Ten Commandments. About seven hundred years after God made that covenant with Israel, God spoke to Jeremiah and said a new covenant was coming that would be written on the people's hearts. In other words God was going to have a more intimate relationship with his people. When you consider your relationship with God, is it a relationship of rules or does it come from your heart? How do you allow God to speak to your heart?

Dear Jesus, you have revealed a personal side of your relationship with us by calling us friends. Help us relate to you and your Father as loving persons who speak to us through our hearts.

▸ To go deeper: Read "The Heart of the Matter" near Jeremiah 31:31–34 in the *CYB*.

Is God Happy with Us?

"This is my Son, my Beloved, with whom I am well pleased."

(2 Peter 1:17)

On the feast of the Transfiguration, we read of God's great affirmation of his Son, Jesus. God declared in front of Peter, James, and John that he was proud of Jesus and his mission in the world. If you decided to go away for a while with three friends, whom would you choose? Once away, imagine you heard God's voice. He calls you his loved one and says he is pleased with you. To what would God be referring? With which of your actions in the last week is God most pleased?

Think of actions you can do with others that would be most pleasing to God. Pray that you will have the strength to do them.

▸ To go deeper: Read "Spiritual Highs" near Luke 9:28–36 in the *CYB*.

Silence Is Golden

"Go out and stand on the mountain
. . . for the LORD is about to pass
by." Now there was a great wind . . .
but the LORD was not in the wind;
and after the wind an earthquake, but
the LORD was not in the earthquake;
and after the earthquake a fire, but the
LORD was not in the fire; and after the
fire a sound of sheer silence.

(1 Kings 19:11–12)

In the silence before the cave, Elijah heard God's voice.
This reminds us that God is generally not going to speak
to us in some dramatic way, but rather in the silence of
our hearts. To hear God, sometimes we need to find a
quiet place—a place without music, radio, television, cell
phones, or DVDs: only silence. There, once we quiet
ourselves and become attuned to how God speaks to us,
we will hear him. As you listen to God, what is he
affirming in you? What is he challenging you to do?

*Lord God, you helped Elijah learn how to listen to you. Now help
me to hear your voice in the silence of my heart through the power of
your Spirit.*

▸ To go deeper: Read "Looking for God" near 1 Kings
  19:9–13 in the *CYB*.

Saint Dominic

So now, O Israel, what does the LORD
your God require of you? . . . To
walk in all [God's] ways, to love him,
to serve the LORD your God with all
your heart and with all your soul, and
to keep the commandments of the
LORD.

(Deuteronomy 10:12–13)

Saint Dominic lived in the twelfth century and founded a
religious community whose goal was to search out and
live by the truth. He was a successful preacher who helped
people know what God required of them. Think of
specific ways in which you walk the right path, love God,
serve him, and keep his commandments. Dominic
preached not only with words but by example. Forgetting
any words you may use about God, reflect on how you
preach about God's love and presence by your lifestyle.

*Dear Jesus, strengthen me to follow the example of Saint Dominic
and study about God, reflect on the Scriptures, and be an example
of a true disciple by my actions.*

▶ To go deeper: Read "Kwanzaa as a Way of Life" near
Deuteronomy 10:12–22 in the *CYB*.

What Never Fails?

> "Do not be afraid, little flock, for it is your Father's good pleasure to give you the kingdom. Sell your possessions, and give alms. Make purses for yourselves that do not wear out."
>
> (Luke 12:32–33)

The Gospels often remind us that material things are not what life is about. We need to focus on the things that keep forever—things that won't be stolen or eaten by moths. Luke challenges us to believe that God will give us what is truly important if we are willing to let go of our need to have things and willing to share what we have with poor people. Think of all the things you have, and decide what you can get rid of to live a simpler life. Either sell the items and give the money to a worthy cause or give the items to an organization that will make good use of them.

Living Spirit of God, give me the courage to get rid of things that distract me from what is really important in life. Help me to focus on building the Reign of God.

▸ To go deeper: Read "The Anxiety Trap" near Luke 12:22–34 in the *CYB*.

Give All You Have!

The point is this: the one who sows
sparingly will also reap sparingly, and
the one who sows bountifully will also
reap bountifully.

(2 Corinthians 9:6)

Saint Paul reminds us that the mission of living out the
Gospel is not for the timid. It is not for those who give
the minimum. It is for those who are willing to take risks
to give all they can, to be on mission 24-7. These are the
disciples who will be successful and accomplish much for
the sake of the Kingdom. If you give a little, you will
receive a little in return; if you give all you, you will
receive even more than you have given. What does that
mean in your life? In what areas are you giving 100
percent? Where are you slacking off? Where do you need
more commitment? more energy?

*Dear Jesus, some days I am really on target with my mission. I am
focused in school. I help at home. I care for my friends. Other times
I'm in a funk and do nothing. Inspire me to keep on keeping on!*

▸ To go deeper: Read 2 Corinthians 9:1–15.

Where Is Jesus Christ?

"For where two or three are gathered
in my name, I am there among them."
(Matthew 18:20)

Sometimes we forget that when we gather in Christ's
name, he is with us. When do we gather in his name?
Anytime we come together to pray, to praise God, to ask
for forgiveness, to celebrate the Eucharist, to remember
the dead, and to support one another in a tragedy, Christ
is with us. Knowing this should encourage us to spend
time praying and sharing with others about Jesus and how
we can share in his mission.

*Lord God, sometimes you seem so far away, so removed. Help me to
remember that your Son, Jesus Christ, is with us when we gather in
his name, and give me the desire to pray and share with others.*

▶ To go deeper: Read Matthew 18:10–20.

Steadfast Love

O give thanks to the LORD, for he is
        good,
    for his steadfast love endures
            forever.

(Psalm 136:1)

The psalmist realized that one of God's unique character-
istics is that he is steadfast. His love is not dependent on
how he feels from one day to the next. It is not like
human love, which can be fickle and not enduring. We
thank God because he is good and his love is everlasting.
What examples of human love do you know that are not
lasting? Which ones seem to last a lifetime? What
difference does it make in your life that God's love is
steadfast?

*Lord God, I know you love me. You love me when I reflect the
values of your Son and when I don't. Enable me to be more steadfast
in my love of others, not here one day and gone the next.*

▸ To go deeper: Read and pray Psalm 136.

Down and Out

> Yes, thus says the Lord GOD: I will deal with you as you have done, you who have despised the oath, breaking the covenant; yet I will remember my covenant with you in the days of your youth, and I will establish with you an everlasting covenant.
>
> (Ezekiel 16:59–60)

Ezekiel writes of God's faithfulness to Israel despite Israel's breaking the covenant with God. God keeps on coming back to us as he did with Israel. Even after we have sinned and abandoned our commitment to God, he seeks to reestablish a relationship with us. How would you describe your covenantal commitment to God? What promises have you made to him? When have you broken those promises? How have you handled that? How would you describe your relationship with God currently?

God, my loving Father, you have been steadfast in your love for me, but I have not been as faithful. Empower me to continue to bond with you by keeping the commitments that Jesus asks of us.

▸ To go deeper: Read "Irresponsible Children" near Ezekiel 23:1–21 in the *CYB*.

Who Is Blessed?

A woman in the crowd raised her voice and said to him, "Blessed is the womb that bore you and the breasts that nursed you!" But he said, "Blessed rather are those who hear the word of God and obey it."

(Luke 11:27–28)

People were so enthusiastic about Jesus's preaching and healings that they thought his mother must be very special. But Jesus made it clear that his mother, Mary, was not blessed because she bore him, but because she heard God's word and kept it. All of us are blessed when we hear God's word and keep it. Jesus is saying that holiness is open to all generations, to all who hear his word, not just to those who had physical contact with him in Judea or Galilee. Where do you regularly hear God's word? How do you keep it?

Dear Jesus, you have proclaimed that I can be blessed, be holy, if I hear your word and keep it. Help me to be attentive to your word at Sunday Mass so that I may live it during the week.

▶ To go deeper: Read "Mary Has a Vital Mission in Salvation History!" near Revelation, chapter 12 in the *CYB*.

The Assumption of Mary

"My soul magnifies the Lord
. . . .
for he has looked with favor on the
lowliness of his servant.
Surely, from now on all generations
will call me blessed;
for the Mighty One has done great
things for me,
and holy is his name."

(Luke 1:46–49)

Mary's yes to God's call made it possible for us to experience a human God, a God with flesh and bones, a God who showed us how much he loved us by giving up his life for us. But Mary is not looking for credit for herself. She is pointing to God for the great things he has done for her, and ultimately for us. She sets an example for us. When you do well at sports or in school, say, "Thank you, God, for blessing me with this talent." Or, when you are recognized for a special accomplishment, point to God as the source of all our blessings and gifts.

Lord God, you looked with favor on Mary because she gave you her unconditional yes. I believe you also look with favor on me. Please help me point to you in all I do, as Mary does.

▸ To go deeper: Read "The Magnificat, the Prayer of the Poor!" near Luke 1:39–56 in the *CYB*.

Peace

Then Gideon built an altar there to the LORD, and called it, The LORD is peace.

(Judges 6:24)

Despite the many violent conflicts in the Old Testament, God's message is always one of peace. Jesus's message, especially after his Resurrection, is always one of peace. Peace is more than the absence of war. Peace is the weaving of diverse strands of life into a harmonious fabric in which every person is strengthened and affirmed. Where do you experience tension or a lack of harmony in your life? in your community? in the world? How can you help people see and appreciate diverse points of view?

Jesus Christ, after the Resurrection, when you met people you always wished them peace. Continue to help promote peace and understanding among the diverse people of the world today.

▶ To go deeper: Read and pray "Trusting God" near Judges 6:36–40 in the *CYB*.

Eye of a Needle

> Then Jesus said to his disciples, "Truly I tell you, it will be hard for a rich person to enter the kingdom of heaven. . . . It is easier for a camel to go through the eye of a needle than for someone who is rich to enter the kingdom of God."
>
> (Matthew 19:23–24)

The city of Jerusalem is a walled city. One gate is very small; camels cannot fit through it. It is only big enough for people to walk through. This gate was called the "eye of the needle." In this passage Jesus is probably referring to that gate, rather than the eye of a sewing needle. The point is that it is hard for people who totally focus on wealth to get to heaven. If all you focus on is getting richer and richer, you probably are not focusing on building God's Kingdom. You will not be using your talents to love God, work for justice, or help your neighbor.

How much time and energy do you spend expanding your wealth or thinking about it? How much time do you spend building the Reign of God? Make an action plan to spend more time on the latter!

▸ To go deeper: Read "The Loaded Question" near Luke 18:18–30 in the *CYB*.

Life Is Not Fair!

> "'These last worked only one hour, and you have made them equal to us who have borne the burden of the day.' . . . But he replied, . . . 'Friend, I am doing you no wrong. . . . So the last will be first, and the first will be last.'"
>
> (Matthew 20:12–16)

In the famous story of the laborers in the vineyard, the owner pays all the workers the same amount, whether they worked all day or only an hour. Those who worked all day got the agreed upon wage, so no injustice was done to them. The others got a generous gift. Of course, that seemed unfair to some. Jesus points out that the owner can be as generous as he wants. He chastises the unhappy workers for being envious of the owner's generosity. When has life seemed unfair to you? Is it really unfair, or are some people being treated differently because of a special reason?

God of justice, assist me in not being judgmental about who is treated fairly and who is not. Empower me to focus on being fair and generous in all my dealings with others.

▸ To go deeper: Pray "Are You for Real?" near Matthew 20:1–16 in the *CYB*.

Wherever You Go

> But Ruth said,
> > "Do not press me to leave you
> > > or to turn back from following
> > > > you!
> > Where you go, I will go;
> > > where you lodge, I will lodge;
> > your people shall be my people,
> > > and your God my God."
>
> (Ruth 1:16)

Ruth was King David's great-grandmother, yet she was not born an Israelite. Her story is in the Bible because of her faithfulness to her Israelite mother-in-law, Naomi. The story of Ruth is one of love and loyalty. This touching story tells how God worked through the faithfulness of ordinary people to bring about his plan of salvation. It gives us insights into how to treat people who are different from us, whether they are foreigners or people of different races. Think of people in school who are different from you. If you take the time to get to know them, your life will be enriched, as Naomi's was.

Lord God, strengthen me to reach out to people who are different from me. Enable me to see the positive qualities in them and to embrace them as my brothers and sisters. I ask this in Jesus's name.

▶ To go deeper: Read "Bill" near Ruth 2:1–16 in the *CYB*.

Stop Boasting!

"All who exalt themselves will be humbled, and all who humble themselves will be exalted."

(Matthew 23:12)

Jesus chastised the scribes and the Pharisees for pretending to be something they were not. He had no time for hypocrisy. He led by serving others, and he expected his followers and the religious leaders to do the same. Today we are sometimes tempted to be boastful, to pretend we are better than we truly are. Sometimes we may boast about our gifts and accomplishments before others, to make them feel inferior. People who do this are usually fairly insecure themselves. Jesus wants you to use your gifts well for the sake of the community, but not with a dominating, boastful attitude.

Jesus, my Lord, help me to know the gifts I have and to use them for the good of others in a humble manner. Never let me take a holier-than-thou attitude; let me have a humble respect for all people.

▸ To go deeper: Read "No Respect" near Matthew 23:1–36 in the *CYB.*

Glory to God

O the depth of the riches and wisdom
and knowledge of God! How un-
searchable are his judgments and how
inscrutable his ways! . . . For from
him and through him and to him are
all things. To him be the glory forever.
Amen.

(Romans 11:33–36)

Paul, in his letter to the Romans, takes time out from his
instruction to praise God. It is as if he can't find enough
superlatives to describe God. Throughout history artists
have attempted to describe God and his works in poetry,
music, and paintings. You may have heard Handel's
Messiah, which praises Jesus Christ and is often performed
during Advent. Reflect on the magnificent images of God
you have read in Paul's writings and have seen or heard in
other artists' portrayals. Add some of your own images as
you pray in praise for the wonders of God.

*Examine the Gospels or Paul's letters for your top five favorite titles
for Jesus Christ. Use the titles in your own prayer.*

▶ To go deeper: Read "The Fate of Israel" near Romans,
chapter 10 in the *CYB.*

Discipline at the Root of Discipleship

Now, discipline always seems painful rather than pleasant at the time, but later it yields the peaceful fruit of righteousness to those who have been trained by it.

(Hebrews 12:11)

Discipline is important for growth in the Christian life. As young adults you are still subject to parental discipline, plus school discipline, and maybe discipline from employers. More and more you are learning self-discipline, that is, you know what you need to do and why you need to do it. It is sometimes challenging to have the self-discipline needed to be good students, respectful sons and daughters, and hard-working employees. Just remember Saint Paul's teaching that discipline is not pleasant, but it bears good fruit.

Jesus, my model and friend, give me the desire to be disciplined in my approach to life. Enable me to develop an inner sense of self-discipline as I mature in discipleship.

▶ To go deeper: Read Hebrews 12:1–13.

Things Are Looking Up!

> We must always give thanks to God
> for you, brothers and sisters, as is
> right, because your faith is growing
> abundantly, and the love of everyone
> of you for one another is increasing.
>
> (2 Thessalonians 1:3)

Saint Paul is feeling very positive about the Thessalonians. Notice how faith and love we have for one another are intimately connected. When we grow in faith, we grow in our love for others. When we grow in our love for others, we grow in our faith. As you look at your circle of friends and at your parish community, what evidence do you see of growth in faith and love? If Paul were writing to you today, what would his opening words be?

Dear Jesus, help me to grow in faith and to believe that I can contribute to your mission on earth. Empower me to grow in love for all people and to show evidence of this by my treatment of others.

▸ To go deeper: Read "Laziness" near 2 Thessalonians 3:6–13 in the *CYB.*

Compassion Wanted!

The LORD is good to all,
> and his compassion is over all that
> > he has made.
All your works shall give thanks to
> you, O LORD,
> and all your faithful shall bless you.
> > (Psalm 145:9–10)

God's love is always connected to his compassion. To be compassionate means to put yourself in the shoes of another person so that you can truly understand that person and all he or she is going through. It implies going the extra mile for another. Apathy is the opposite of compassion; it means closing your heart to others. Compassion means reaching out to an ill person, supporting someone who is down, forgiving what seems to be unforgivable, spending time with a person who feels isolated, and embracing someone who is ostracized by others.

God of compassion, enable me to walk in the shoes of another so that I can best understand how to support that person. Especially help me to do this with those who are isolated from others.

▶ To go deeper: Read and pray Psalm 145.

The Pretenders

"Woe to you, scribes and Pharisees,
hypocrites! For you clean the outside
of the cup and of the plate, but inside
they are full of greed and self-
indulgence."

(Matthew 23:25)

Jesus was really going after the pretenders—those who
project goodness but really are sinful. He had no time for
hypocrites. Sometimes people look terrific and appear to
be nice, but are conniving and manipulative. They use
others under the pretense of helping them. We do the
same when we do extra chores around the house only
when we want a parent or sibling to do us a favor. Or
when we act especially nice only when we want to be
noticed by someone special. Jesus tells us we need to be
consistent in the good we do, not just turn it on when we
want something for ourselves!

*Lord Jesus, help me to know who I am and to become who you want
me to be. Strengthen me to avoid hypocrisy and not to practice
goodness only when it's convenient for me.*

▸ To go deeper: Read Matthew 23:1–36.

Be Watchful

> "Keep awake therefore, for you do not
> know on what day your Lord is
> coming."
>
> (Matthew 24:42)

Sometimes we think we will live forever and we will have
a lot of time to prepare for heaven. People asked Jesus
when the end of the world would come or when the Son
of Man would come to judge all people. In response, Jesus
told parables that pointed to the fact that we always need
to be watchful, because we do not know when God will
call us to eternal life. In other words we need to live each
day as if it were our last. We are sometimes reminded of
the shortness of life when we hear of car accidents or the
sudden death of a friend. We need to be proud of our
actions toward God and others each day.

*Imagine that you were told you had twenty-four hours to live. What
would you do with the time? Knowing that any day could be your
last day, what do you wish to change in your life now?*

▸ To go deeper: Pray "When Are You Coming?" near Matthew
25:1–13 in the *CYB*.

Slow to Anger

The LORD is merciful and gracious,
    slow to anger and abounding in
        steadfast love.
He will not always accuse,
    nor will he keep his anger forever.
                    (Psalm 103:8–9)

Read these lines again, looking at the beautiful qualities we
are told that God has. These qualities are wonderful goals
for us to strive for in our own life. You can use each one
of them for your own meditation: When have you been
merciful? With whom can you show mercy? When have
you been slow to anger? With whom do you need to be
more patient? Whom do you faithfully love? To whom do
you need to be more faithful? Take a few minutes to
reflect on how you embody these qualities of God. It
could change your life!

*O God who loves me so much, I am so grateful that you are merciful
when I fail in my words and actions. I want to exercise the same
qualities in my treatment of others that you have with me.*

▸ To go deeper: Read "Letting Go of Anger" near Psalm 103
  in the *CYB*.

Discipleship

> Then Jesus told his disciples, "If any want to become my followers, let them deny themselves and take up their cross and follow me."
>
> (Matthew 16:24)

If we are to follow Jesus, there is no getting away from the cross. Notice Jesus talks not about helping carry his cross, but rather about carrying our own cross. Our crosses can be anything from having a weight problem to being shy to being lonely to not having friends to not having a talent for sports or perhaps academics. Our cross may be living with a parent who is addicted to alcohol, an ill parent, or an "out of control" sibling. No matter what the circumstances may be, we are not going to avoid pain and suffering in our life. The good news is that we are empowered by the Spirit to be able to carry our crosses.

Lord Jesus, as you know, crosses are hard to carry. Please strengthen me to carry my crosses with a positive attitude, knowing that in doing so I am growing closer to you.

▶ To go deeper: Read "The Principle of *Ujamaa*" near Matthew 16:25 in the *CYB*.

Use Your Common Sense

Jesus asked, . . . "Is it lawful to cure people on the sabbath, or not?" . . . Then he said to them, "If one of you has a child or an ox that has fallen into a well, will you not immediately pull it out on a sabbath day?"

(Luke 14:3–5)

The Pharisees, who had a negative attitude toward Jesus, were always watching him to see if they could catch him doing something against the law. In this case Jesus raises the question that was on their minds. They have no answer to his question. So Jesus answers his own question with the example of a child or an animal that has fallen in a well. The answer is pretty obvious; there is nothing the Pharisees can say. We sometimes face people who challenge our beliefs and practices. You can be as wise in your response as Jesus was if you keep focused on this question: "What does true love require?"

Dear Jesus, you faced many tensions in your life about the way you lived your religious values. Help me to be as wise as you in answering challenges to my faith.

▶ To go deeper: Read Luke 14:1–6.

So You Think You Are Important!

> "When you are invited, go and sit down at the lowest place, so that when your host comes, he may say to you, 'Friend, move up higher'; then you will be honored in the presence of all."
>
> (Luke 14:10)

Jesus told a parable about someone who thought he was so important that he went to the head of the table, only to be asked to go to the lowest place at the table. He must have been very embarrassed. Jesus's point was that it is better to be asked to come forward to receive an honor than it is to presume we are greater than someone else. Being humble means being in touch with who we are and what our talents are, but at the same time, not assuming we are more important than anyone else. The point is to not focus on who is the greatest. In God's eyes we all are equal.

Name things about yourself for which you are proud. Name areas where you are tempted to exaggerate your abilities. Pray to Jesus for the gift of humility.

▸ To go deeper: Read "God's Invitation List" near Luke 14:7–24 in the *CYB*.

Rejection

And [Jesus] said, "Truly I tell you, no
prophet is accepted in the prophet's
hometown."

(Luke 4:24)

Jesus was preaching in his hometown, Nazareth. The
people were impressed by his preaching. Yet they could
not believe that this local boy was a great prophet, and
they ended up driving him out of town. Sometimes when
we speak the truth, herald a new idea, or try to build a
coalition to attack some social issue, we are rejected. That
hurts. We feel isolated and lonely. We might be tempted to
avoid taking a risk again. However, our model is Jesus, and
he did not back down. He changed his strategy and
looked for people who might listen to and appreciate his
message.

*Jesus, my model and my brother, sustain me as I try to courageously
proclaim your Gospel message through my words and my life's
actions.*

▸ To go deeper: Read "Jesus Liberates People from Oppression!" near Luke 4:14–30 in the *CYB*.

Remembering Your Friends

> For this reason, since the day we heard it, we have not ceased praying for you and asking that you may be filled with the knowledge of God's will . . . so that you may lead lives worthy of the Lord, fully pleasing to him.
>
> (Colossians 1:9–10)

Wendy was moved to tears when she found out that Charlie had taped the names of his best friends to his computer screen so that he would remember to say a quick prayer for them each morning. "Do you know how that makes me feel?" she asked. "Just imagine that someone is praying for me every single day!" For whom might you pray every day? What will help you remember to do that? Is there someone, perhaps a friend or a grandparent, you might ask to pray for you like that?

Saint Paul, you prayed for your friends without ceasing. Help me to remember to pray for my friends today.

▶ To go deeper: Read Colossians 1:1–14.

Working Together

> For as long as there is jealousy and
> quarreling among you, are you not of
> the flesh, and behaving according to
> human inclinations?
>
> (1 Corinthians 3:3)

It is easy to be jealous, to feel that someone is better
looking or stronger or smarter or more popular. Another
team or school or town or country feels like a threat, and
we slip into destructive competition. Sometimes we fall
into jealous behavior without even realizing it. Keeping
our perspective can be hard if we don't have a strong
sense of who we are. We must be constantly on guard
against acting out of jealousy and foolish rivalry. So much
more can be accomplished with cooperation instead of
jealousy and unhealthy competition.

*Dear Jesus, give me a cooperative spirit at home, at school, and at
work. Inspire me to cooperate with, rather than compete with, those
by whom I feel threatened.*

▶ To go deeper: Read "We Are God's Servants, Who Share a
Common Mission!" near 1 Corinthians 3:1–15 in the *CYB*.

Saint Gregory the Great

Think of us in this way, as servants of Christ and stewards of God's mysteries.

(1 Corinthians 4:1)

Gregory was a Benedictine monk who was elected Pope at the age of fifty. Even as a young monk, Gregory knew the importance of prayer to help keep him centered. Gregory lived at a time of great confusion and lawlessness, and he worked for justice and peace. He emptied the treasury to ransom prisoners and removed unworthy priests from office. He was a wise man who cared for persecuted Jews and victims of the plague. He had to make many hard choices during his life, and he relied on the Holy Spirit's gift of wisdom to help him make them.

When you are faced with hard choices or temptations, take a minute to pray, "Come, Holy Spirit."

▸ To go deeper: Read "God's Wisdom and Ours" near 1 Corinthians 1:18–31 in the *CYB*.

Enduring Ridicule

> But let none of you suffer as a
> murderer, a thief, a criminal, or even
> as a mischief maker. Yet if any of you
> suffers as a Christian, do not consider
> it a disgrace, but glorify God because
> you bear this name.
>
> (1 Peter 4:15–16)

It is painful to be made fun of. One of the cruelest things
to witness is someone being humiliated. People can be
ridiculed for as simple a thing as the kind of clothes they
wear or the friends they hang out with. People can also be
ridiculed for going to church, attending religious events,
and taking a stance against war or abortion. Even in a
country that cherishes freedom of thought and expression, many people have narrow attitudes. It takes courage
to endure such ridicule and to keep on being faithful to
your beliefs despite being laughed at for them.

*Dear Jesus, you were unafraid to stand with people that society
ridiculed and dismissed. Help me to have the courage to do the same
when I see someone being put down or made fun of.*

▸ To go deeper: Read "Shout for Joy!" near 1 Peter 4:12–19 in
the *CYB*.

Choose Your Friends Wisely

Make no friends with those given to
     anger,
     and do not associate with hotheads,
or you may learn their ways
     and entangle yourself in a snare.
                    (Proverbs 22:24–25)

People who are smart choose friends who are the kind of people they want to become. It's only natural that we all influence the people we hang out with and that they influence us. The author of the Book of Proverbs knew this, and warned against friends who may have a bad effect on us. It doesn't mean that we shouldn't be friendly with all people, including hotheads. But choose people with good values and a positive outlook on life as your closest friends. Be a person who is positive and that's the kind of friends you will attract.

Holy Spirit, help me to find friends who model the values and attitudes Jesus calls us to have. Help me to be that kind of person for my friends.

▸ To go deeper: Read "Count to Ten" near Proverbs 17:14 in the *CYB*.

Talking with God

> Now during those days he went out to
> the mountain to pray; and he spent
> the night in prayer to God.
>
> (Luke 6:12)

Can you imagine staying up all night to pray? Though we might stay up all night at a prom party or a homecoming celebration, it is rare that we'd do the same to pray. Jesus gave us this example more than once. Through prayer he nurtured the close relationship he had with God the Father. The test of our prayer, however, is not its length—how long we spend in prayer—but our commitment to keeping our relationship with God strong and alive. Take advantage of opportunities like retreats to nurture your prayer life. Maybe even try spending part of a night alone somewhere for your own extended time with God.

Think about your own prayer life and see if you want to make any changes. Talk to a priest or youth minister for suggestions about how you can grow your prayer life.

▶ To go deeper: Read "Renewing Your Prayer Life" near 2 Chronicles 29:3–11 in the *CYB*.

How Can This Be True?

Then he looked up at his disciples and
said:
    "Blessed are you who are poor,
        for yours is the kingdom of
            God."

(Luke 6:20)

"Blessed are you who are poor" sounds like a contradiction. Even when some translations use the phrase "Happy are you who are poor," it still sounds like a contradiction. But many of the Gospel values we are called to embrace and live out contradict what our culture teaches. Jesus always had a special place for the poor, and we are expected to do likewise. Jesus knows that poor people are often happier than wealthy people because they are more aware of their dependence on God. Do you know someone who is poor? What does that person have to teach you about happiness?

Come, Holy Spirit, and never let me forget, whether I am poor or wealthy, that everything I have comes from God. Only in trusting God for what I need can I truly be happy.

▶ To go deeper: Read "Jesus' Preference for the Poor" near Luke 6:17–49 in the *CYB*.

The Nativity of the Blessed Virgin Mary

And those whom [God] predestined
he also called; and those whom he
called he also justified; and those
whom he justified he also glorified
(Romans 8:30)

Today we celebrate Mary's birthday! We can thank God
she was born and she said yes to being the mother of
Jesus. But her birthday was just like that of any other child
in her village. No one thought it was special except her
own family. The same is true with each of us. We are
born. We have no idea what the future will bring for us.
We have no idea of the lives we will touch and the ways
we will be seeds of God's Kingdom of goodness and
justice. We just need to be able to be willing to say yes to
God, as Mary did.

*Write a press release describing your return home after being gone for
ten years. It should not focus on your job accomplishments but rather
on the person you've become and the qualities people see in you.*

▸ To go deeper: Read Romans 8:26–39.

Saint Peter Claver

"That one is like a man building a house, who dug deeply and laid the foundation on rock; when a flood arose, the river burst against that house but could not shake it, because it had been well built."

(Luke 6:48)

Peter Claver was born in Spain and went to Colombia as a missionary to serve the African slaves who were brought there to be sold in America. For years he would meet the ships and bring food and medicine to the slaves, who were herded out in chains to be sold like animals. Peter preached to them of their own goodness and of God's love for them. Not only was Saint Claver's life built on the solid rock of belief in God's love, but he passed that on to those he served.

Pray to Saint Peter Claver to help you continue to build a strong foundation of faith for the times when life is challenging, and to see and reach out to the helpless as he did.

▶ To go deeper: Pray "I Therefore Commit" near Hosea 12:2–6 in the *CYB*.

Win the Prize

Do you not know that in a race the runners all compete, but only one receives the prize? Run in such a way that you may win it.

(1 Corinthians 9:24)

Some people seem to be competitive by nature. Throw any challenge out and they go for it. Other people shy away from competition; they have no desire to be in a win-lose situation. What is your competition quotient? Whatever it is, Saint Paul reminds us that the most important competition we have in life is not against another person or to attain wealth or prestige. It is for the prize we receive for being the best person we can be with the gifts God has placed in us. That prize may be recognized by no one but us and God. We should strive for it every day because it is worth the race.

Dear Jesus, help me to focus my competitive attitude on what truly matters, that is, having the self-discipline to live a life that is pleasing to you and to your heavenly Father.

▸ To go deeper: Read "Spiritual Perseverance" near 1 Corinthians 9:24–27 in the *CYB*.

Christ Is Here

> The cup of blessing that we bless, is it
> not a sharing in the blood of Christ?
> The bread that we break, is it not a
> sharing in the body of Christ?
>
> (1 Corinthians 10:16)

It's Sunday morning, and Mom is calling you to get up to go to church. How much easier it is to turn over under the covers! But what if Jesus was really going to be there today? In fact, he is. Because we have faith, we believe he really is there—in the priest, in the Scriptures we hear, in the consecrated bread and wine, and in the community itself. Hurry and get dressed!

Jesus, I want to believe. Give me eyes of faith. Give me ears to hear. Help me to be open to your presence in all the ways you come to us at Mass.

▸ To go deeper: Read "Called to Share" near 1 Corinthians 11:17–33 in the *CYB*.

I'm Sorry

> "Just so, I tell you, there will be more joy in heaven over one sinner who repents than over ninety-nine righteous persons who need no repentance."
>
> (Luke 15:7)

We all fail sometimes. We don't always do what we know we should, or we do what we know we shouldn't. Then it's over and too late. But it's never too late to be forgiven. It's never too late to say "I'm sorry." God is willing to forgive us before we even are even ready to say "I'm sorry." Not that God needs our sorrow to be complete. But we need a heart that is sorry and willing to say the words "Please forgive me," so that we might be complete. Isn't it wonderful to know that God takes such joy when his creatures take steps to be whole again?

Is there someone to whom you need to say "I'm sorry"? Perhaps you weren't even totally wrong, but things are not all right between you. Go to that person today.

▸ To go deeper: Read "Be Reconciled" near 1 John 2:7–11 in the *CYB*.

Saint John Chrysostom

> For we do not proclaim ourselves; we
> proclaim Jesus Christ as Lord and
> ourselves as your slaves for Jesus's
> sake.
>
> (2 Corinthians 4:5)

Saint John Chrysostom was a bishop who was unpopular
with the rich and powerful people of his time. He lived
simply, and he preached dramatically and concretely that
the rich should share with the poor and that husbands
should be faithful to their wives—both unpopular ideas in
his day. He had no desire to be a bishop and refused to
take part in the politics of the day. John Chrysostom, a
humble person, was clear about who he was and from
whom his power came.

*Whom do you admire, not because they are popular or successful but
because of the kind of people they are? Let them know what you
admire about them.*

▶ To go deeper: Read "Christ in Us" near 2 Corinthians 4:5–10
in the *CYB*.

The Exaltation of the Cross

"And just as Moses lifted up the serpent in the wilderness, so must the Son of Man be lifted up, that whoever believes in him may have eternal life."

(John 3:14–15)

During Lent and Holy Week, we take time to honor the cross. On Good Friday we kiss the cross on which Jesus suffered and died. On today's feast, however, we honor the glorious cross, the symbol of our redemption. Today the cross is to be celebrated and honored because it is viewed in the light of Christ's Resurrection. What joy we can have knowing that because of the cross and the Resurrection, what awaited Jesus in heaven also awaits us! On this feast we are reminded in a concrete way of the great love God has for us.

Come, Holy Spirit, and help me meditate on the cross and remember to thank God for the great gift that awaits us because of Christ's death and Resurrection.

▶ To go deeper: Read Numbers 21:1–9 to see the Old Testament basis of this passage in John.

Our Lady of Sorrows

"This child is destined for the falling and the rising of many in Israel, and to be a sign that will be opposed so that the inner thoughts of many will be revealed—and a sword will pierce your own soul too."

(Luke 2:34–35)

When the holy man Simeon said these words to Mary, Jesus was just a tiny child. We know that his words came true when Mary witnessed the pain and suffering Jesus endured later in life. She was a strong woman to endure all that she did as the mother of Jesus. Parents who are watching their children go through difficult times have a special kinship with Mary. The Catholic Church proclaims Mary as the spiritual mother of all believers. We can go to her to experience her loving care for us and to ask for her strength to hold us up when we have our own kinds of pain.

Before you go to sleep tonight, put all your problems in Mary's care. Ask her to be with all those in the world who are suffering tonight, as she was with her own Son in his suffering.

▸ To go deeper: Read "Living Gospel Values Even if It Demands Suffering!" near 1 Peter 3:13–22 in the *CYB*.

I Am What I Am

But by the grace of God I am what I am, and his grace toward me has not been in vain. On the contrary, I worked harder than any of them— though it was not I, but the grace of God that is with me.

(1 Corinthians 15:10)

The things Saint Paul is saying about himself are also true for each of us. God has created us the way we are. To realize our gifts and talents is not vanity as long as we give God credit for them. To despise who we are or to long to be someone else is to not appreciate that we are God's creation—but appreciating that we are God's creation is often easier to say than to do. Some people get messages from our culture, from other people, sometimes even from a parent that they are not good enough. When you begin to feel that way, remember Saint Paul's words, "By the grace of God I am what I am, and his grace toward me has not been in vain."

God of all creation, sometimes it is easy to forget that I am your wonderful creation. Help me have a grateful heart and an acceptance of who I am.

▸ To go deeper: Read "The First Creed and a Contemporary Creed!" near 1 Corinthians 15:3–11.

Saint Robert Bellarmine

"Now, the parable is this: The seed is the word of God. . . . But as for that in the good soil, these are the ones who, when they hear the word, hold it fast in an honest and good heart, and bear fruit with patient endurance."

(Luke 8:11–15)

Saint Robert Bellarmine was a theologian and Scripture scholar. He was a Jesuit priest who was made a cardinal because the Pope said, "He had not his equal for learning." In spite of his brilliance and honors, Robert ate only the food available to the poor and used the hangings in his room to clothe poor people. He said, "The walls won't catch cold." The seed of God's word found good soil in Robert Bellarmine.

Pray to Saint Robert Bellarmine that your heart and mind will be good soil for the word of God. Pray that you may put the lessons of the Gospel into action in your life as he did in his.

▶ To go deeper: Read Luke 8:4–15.

You Love Me This Much?

> "'Take what belongs to you and go; I
> choose to give to this last the same as
> I give to you. Am I not allowed to do
> what I choose with what belongs to
> me?'"
>
> (Matthew 20:14–15)

The hired hands who worked all day wanted more money
than they'd agreed to because latecomers received the
same amount as they did. The generosity of the vineyard
owner was resented, though the workers were paid a fair
wage. We, too, should be careful that we do not fall into
the trap of feeling that God owes us something. Each of
us has sinned and broken our commitments to God. The
good news is that our God is even more generous to us
than the vineyard owner was to the latecomers! In fact,
the generous love of God is more than we can ever
imagine.

*God of infinite love, thank you for not giving up on me but
continuing to love me even when I do not deserve your love. I praise
you for being more generous with your love than I could ever imagine.*

▸ To go deeper: Pray "Can You Hear Me, Lord?" near Luke
18:1–8 in the *CYB*.

Staying Faithful

"Whoever is faithful in a very little is faithful also in much; and whoever is dishonest in a very little is dishonest also in much."

(Luke 16:10)

Did you ever notice that sometimes it's easier to do the right thing when it's something big than when it's something small? We might talk ourselves into believing that cheating a little or lying a little or even stealing a little isn't that bad. After all, we'd never do anything seriously wrong. The Gospel verse here is saying to beware of that kind of thinking. How we act in little things is a sign of how we act in important things.

Be with me, Lord, when I am tempted to do wrong in small things. Let me remember these words from Luke's Gospel and have the courage to do what is right.

▶ To go deeper: Read "Understanding Parables" near Luke 16:1–13 in the *CYB*.

Andrew Kim Taegon, Paul Chong Hasang, and Companions

> "No one after lighting a lamp hides it under a jar, or puts it under a bed, but puts it on a lampstand, so that those who enter may see the light."
>
> (Luke 8:16)

When a Chinese priest secretly entered Korea in 1789, he found four thousand Catholics there. None of them had ever seen a priest. It was a lay church. Korea didn't have religious freedom for nearly another century. These laypeople had spread the Catholic faith completely on their own. Many of them were cruelly tortured and killed for it. They are the martyrs whose feast day is celebrated today. How fortunate we are to have freedom of religion at no cost to us when many have been killed just for believing.

Decide today on one way to take the lamp of your faith and put it on a lampstand. You might wear a cross, carry your prayer book or Bible openly, or invite someone to go to church with you.

▸ To go deeper: Pray "Prayer for Roots and Faith" near Luke 8:4–15 in the *CYB*.

Saint Matthew,
Apostle and Evangelist

As Jesus was walking along, he saw a man called Matthew sitting at the tax booth; and he said to him, "Follow me." And he got up and followed him.

(Matthew 9:9)

Matthew was a Jew who collected taxes for the Romans, who occupied Israel during the life of Jesus. The tax collectors were usually hated by their fellow Jews. Some strict Jews like the Pharisees considered tax collectors to be sinners because they handled Roman currency that had on it the image of Caesar—which the Pharisees considered to be idolatry. Thus many people were shocked when Jesus chose Matthew to be one of his closest followers. By choosing Matthew, Jesus shows us that no one is beyond hearing and responding to God's call.

Dear Jesus, help me hear your call as clearly as Matthew heard it sitting at his work that day, and help me respond as quickly and completely as he responded.

▸ To go deeper: Read the introduction to the Gospel According to Matthew in the *CYB*.

Before I Die

> Two things I ask of you;
>> do not deny them to me before I
>>> die:
> Remove far from me falsehood and
>> lying;
>> give me neither poverty nor riches;
>> feed me with the food that I need.
>
> (Proverbs 30:7–8)

This wisdom saying of Agur in the Book of Proverbs gives us pause today as it did then. Having lived a long life, he now is asking to receive what he has figured out is most important. He does not want lies, but the truth. He does not want to be rich or poor because either might lead him away from God. He only wants the food that he needs. What nourishment do you want to feed you to allow you to live a good life? Is it wisdom, integrity, honesty, love of others? Is it fame or fortune? Is it safety, peace, or family and friends? A wise person knows the things that will lead us to God and the things that will lead us away from God.

Come, Holy Spirit, and give me the gift of wisdom so that I might choose those things that will lead me toward God and avoid those things that will lead me away from him.

▸ To go deeper: Read "Wisdom and the Elders" near Proverbs 24:3–4 in the *CYB*.

Such Great Love

Do not fear, for I have redeemed you;
I have called you by name, you are
mine.

(Isaiah 43:1)

As a young child, do you remember being afraid of the
dark or of strange noises? When they are afraid, many
young children run to their parents to find security in
their love. This gets harder to do as we grow older—but
not impossible! Yet even a parent's love pales in comparison to how God loves each one of us. And God loves no
one more than he loves you. That thought can be
overwhelming and it can also give you courage and take
away fear. Our best response to that love is to let go of
our fears and be courageous in serving others.

*You formed me, God, and redeemed me. Yet I still have fears and
anxieties. Let me find safety and courage in your loving care for me.*

▶ To go deeper: Read "Be Not Afraid" near Isaiah 43:1–5 in
the *CYB*.

Everything Has Its Time

For everything there is a season, and a time for every matter under heaven.

(Ecclesiastes 3:1)

Change happens. In our life we have times of joy and times of sorrow, times of letting go and times of holding on, times of moving forward and times of looking back. We cannot see the front of the tapestry we are weaving with our life. We can only see the back, which may look like tangled, unconnected threads. It is up to us to weave all the good and bad times by keeping our focus on Jesus Christ. Ultimately our faith in Christ will help us make sense of what is happening now, especially when we can't imagine what the reason may be. It may take a lifetime, though, to see that reason.

Dear Jesus, sometimes things are clear and sometimes they are confused. Sometimes everything works together and sometimes everything falls apart. Through it all help me to keep my eyes on you.

▸ To go deeper: Pray "The Balance of Life" near Ecclesiastes 3:1–8 in the *CYB*.

We Need One Another

Remember your creator in the days of your youth, before the days of trouble come, and the years draw near when you will say, "I have no pleasure in them."

(Ecclesiastes 12:1)

Ecclesiastes tells us that it is good to be young. Though there may be problems and challenges, it is a time of strength and hope and looking to the future. Aging brings its own joys in life accomplishments, in pleasant memories, and in wisdom. But for many elderly people, it is a difficult time of letting go of their health, their friends, and even their independence. You have a great gift to give them: your presence and your time. They have wisdom and experience to offer you.

Reach out to the elderly people in your family, your neighborhood, and your church. Visit with people in a nursing home. You'd be amazed at how much a warm hello can mean to an elderly person.

▸ To go deeper: Read "Remember the Elderly" near Ecclesiastes 12:1–8 in the *CYB*.

Saints Cosmos and Damian

> Honor physicians for their services,
>   for the Lord created them;
> for their gift of healing comes from
>   the Most High.
>
> (Sirach 38:1–2)

Cosmos and Damian were killed for their Christian faith. Other than the fact that they were martyrs, we know little about them. Legend says that they were twins who were skilled doctors in Arabia. They are venerated in that part of the world as "the moneyless ones" because they took care of poor people and didn't charge for their medical services. People who provide health care for others share in a special way in Christ's healing ministry.

Jesus, divine healer, bless all the doctors, nurses, aides, and technicians who continue your healing ministry. Give them patience and compassion as they face the challenges of caring for others.

▶ To go deeper: Read "Health-Care Providers" near Sirach 38:1–15 in the *CYB*.

Saint Vincent de Paul

"Whoever welcomes this child in my name welcomes me, and whoever welcomes me welcomes the one who sent me; for the least among all of you is the greatest."

(Luke 9:48)

Saint Vincent de Paul was a farm boy in France who grew up, became a priest, and expected to live a quiet life. However, his eyes were opened to the spiritual and physical needs of the French peasants. When he was sent to Paris to minister, he organized the wealthy women there to collect funds for his projects, which included hospitals for the poor, relief funds for war victims, and paying for the freedom of over twelve hundred African slaves. During the course of his life, Vincent took Jesus' words seriously and ministered to those considered the "least among all of you."

Volunteer this week in a soup kitchen, a food bank, a homeless shelter, or anyplace Jesus would call the people there "the greatest."

▸ To go deeper: Read "Stand Up and Be Counted!" near Amos 8:4–8 in the *CYB*.

Bad Things Happen

"Let the day perish in which I was
      born,
   and the night that said,
   'A man-child is conceived.'"

(Job 3:3)

Poor Job lost so much in his life, and he had a lot to lose. He felt angry and depressed in his suffering—as you can see from the above quote—but he never lost his faith in God. And he did not give in to the temptation to think that God must be punishing him for some secret sin, even though others tried to convince him that that was the problem. You probably know people who have had bad things happen to them through no fault of their own: they have a severe illness, their parents divorced, a family member dies. We can support them with our presence and reassure them that God is not punishing them.

Reach out to anyone you know who is discouraged, sad, or angry at what is happening in their life. Even if you don't know exactly what to say, let them know they are not alone.

▶ To go deeper: Read "In Good Times and Bad" near Job 1:13–21 in the *CYB*.

Michael, Gabriel, and Raphael, Archangels

And he said to him, "Very truly, I tell you, you will see heaven opened and the angels of God ascending and descending upon the Son of Man."

(John 1:51)

Angels are God's messengers. They appear often in the Bible, but only these three are named. Gabriel is the most well known, as he is the messenger who asks Mary, the young Jewish girl, to bear the Messiah. In the Scriptures each of these three has a different role: Michael protects, Gabriel announces, and Raphael guides. God's messengers are important in everyone's life. God has many ways of speaking to us, whether it is a friend telling us of a good quality or talent they see in us or a complete stranger with a message of hope and encouragement when we most need it.

Heavenly Father, help me pay attention to the messengers you send to me, both those who are easily recognized and those who may not be so obvious.

▶ To go deeper: Read "Angels Among Us" near Tobit, chapter 8 in the *CYB*.

Saint Jerome

"O that my words were written down!
  O that they were inscribed in a
    book!
O that with an iron pen and with lead
    they were engraved on a rock
      forever!"

(Job 19:23–24)

What Job wished for in this Scripture passage was certainly true for Saint Jerome. Jerome, a Scripture scholar, translated most of the Old Testament from Hebrew. He also wrote commentaries on the Bible that are still used today. In order to do this work, he took his studies seriously. Jerome also had little patience for religious leaders who thought more about worldly things than about the true spiritual life. Faced with people who were spreading false truths, he often challenged them with a sarcastic tongue that got him into trouble. Yet Saint Jerome's personal holiness was clear to all, and he has been declared a doctor of the Church.

Pray to Saint Jerome, the student, to help you take your studies seriously. Pray to Saint Jerome, the writer, to help you choose your words carefully, especially when you are angry.

▸ To go deeper: Read and pray "Tripping Over My Tongue" near Matthew 12:33–37 in the *CYB*.

Saint Thérèse of Lisieux

> At the same hour Jesus rejoiced in the Holy Spirit and said, "I thank you, Father, Lord of heaven and earth, because you have hidden these things from the wise and the intelligent and have revealed them to infants; yes, Father, for such was your gracious will."
>
> (Luke 10:21)

The "little flower," as Saint Thérèse was often called, had great insights into the simplicity of life and how small things pleased God. Her mother died when she was young, and Therese entered a convent at only fourteen years old. She lived to be only twenty-four. She grasped the importance of being as gentle and loving as possible in overcoming the little trials of life. Jesus, too, points to the simplicity of God's message. One does not need to be a learned theologian to understand the Gospel. If you were asked to summarize the message of the Gospel in one sentence, what would it be?

Lord Jesus, help me to understand the simplicity of your message and apply it to my life in everyday things with the same determination that Saint Thérèse had.

▸ To go deeper: Pray "A Prayer for the Young" near Psalm 144 in the *CYB*.

Guardian Angels

> Then turning to the disciples, Jesus
> said to them privately, "Blessed are the
> eyes that see what you see!"
>
> (Luke 10:23)

Guardian angels protect us. We can't see them, but we
believe that God has created them. They are spirits who
care for us and give us nudges when we need them. In the
passage from Luke, Jesus is blessing people who see with
the eyes of faith, for it takes faith to believe in angels and
it takes angels to help us be faith-filled disciples of Christ.
Are you conscious of your guardian angel? Do you ask
your angel for guidance, for protection? When has your
guardian angel seemed most present to you?

Holy Spirit, help me to be more aware of my guardian angel.
Enable me to ask for my angel's help and protection now and when
I am in trouble.

▸ To go deeper: Read "Entertaining Angels" near Hebrews
13:1–5 in the *CYB*.

Doing the Minimum

> "We are worthless slaves; we have done only what we ought to have done!"
>
> (Luke 17:10)

In this verse Jesus warns his disciples not to think too highly of themselves just because they are doing what he asks. Some people want to do only the minimum needed to get by. They don't go out of their way to be helpful to others. Sometimes young people are like that. Let's say their job is to take the garbage out after dinner. On a weekend they ignore the fact that the bag is full and needs to be taken out at noon. They pretend they don't see that the recycling bin needs to be emptied. They do what is literally expected, nothing more. When are you tempted to be a minimalist? How can you change that attitude?

Look at all the things you need to do. Choose three of them and develop an action plan on how you can enrich people's lives by doing more that what is expected.

▶ To go deeper: Read Luke 17:1–10.

Saint Francis of Assisi

"Which of these three, do you think, was a neighbor to the man who fell into the hands of the robbers?" He said, "The one who showed him mercy." Jesus said to him, "Go and do likewise."

(Luke 10:36–37)

Saint Francis of Assisi is an example of a person who was a good neighbor. He came from a wealthy family but gave up his wealth for the good of others. In the parable of the good Samaritan, we have a story about the least likely person, a Samaritan, acting as a true neighbor. Samaritans were despised by the Jews. But in the story, a priest and a Levite (a respected Jewish leader) ignored an injured man. Only the Samaritan stopped to help. The Samaritan and Saint Francis have much in common. They both went out of their way to help others. They were both willing to be inconvenienced to help others.

Dear Jesus, I wish to be as compassionate toward others as were the good Samaritan and Saint Francis. Give me a spirit that is willing to sacrifice some of my own needs to help others.

▸ To go deeper: Read "Discrimination in Jesus' Time" near Luke 10:25–37 in the *CYB*.

So Is It Work or Prayer?

> "Martha, Martha, you are worried and distracted by many things; there is need of only one thing. Mary has chosen the better part, which will not be taken away from her."
>
> (Luke 10:41–42)

In this story Martha is complaining to Jesus that her sister, Mary, is not helping with the chores. Instead Mary sits and listens to Jesus. Jesus challenges Martha to look at what is really important in life and spend her time at that. Jesus's message is not about who should be in the kitchen; it is about women hearing God's word. At the time of Jesus, women were not allowed into the inner part of the temple and had to listen to the readings from behind a screen or from the courtyard. Jesus is changing that and is helping Martha and Mary see that they are allowed direct access to God's word through him.

Jesus, you broke through the divisions of social class, race, and gender so that all people would know God's love. Help me to respect each person I meet as completely as you did.

▸ To go deeper: Read "The Silent Women of the Bible" near Esther 4:15–17 in the *CYB*.

Poverty

> They asked only one thing, that we
> remember the poor, which was
> actually what I was eager to do.
>
> (Galatians 2:10)

Paul was checking out his mission with the other Apostles. He discovered that he was on the right track. The only thing Peter asked him to do was to be sure to remember the poor. Two thousand years later, that challenge still remains before us. Every Christian, young and old, is responsible for taking care of poor people. Our response must be twofold. First we must do what we can to meet people's immediate physical needs. But second, we must study the causes of poverty and do what we can to eliminate the reasons for homelessness, hunger, and all forms of poverty.

Do some research on the causes of local poverty. Work with a group of your classmates to take some practical steps to reduce poverty. Pray to the Holy Spirit for guidance.

▸ To go deeper: Read "Consistent and Trustworthy" near Galatians 2:11–14 in the *CYB*.

Nag a Little

"For everyone who asks receives, and everyone who searches finds, and for everyone who knocks, the door will be opened."

(Luke 11:10)

Sometimes we have to get assertive and be persistent with God. Jesus reminds us that we need to ask for our needs. We need to search out answers. We need to knock—and sometimes pound—to get the door open. With this encouragement we need to examine what we are really asking for and how important it is in our lives. To ask for trivial material things may show that we are focusing on personal wants instead of real needs. Those things tend to quickly fade away, while growth in values and relationships lasts forever.

Dear Jesus, now that you have encouraged me to be persistent in asking God to have my needs met, strengthen me to ask for what is really important and what will last a lifetime.

▸ To go deeper: Read "Nagging God" near Luke 11:5–13 in the *CYB*.

The Beauty of Creation

The Lord is king! Let the earth rejoice;
  let the many coastlands be glad!
Clouds and the thick darkness are all
    around him;
  righteousness and justice are the
    foundation of his throne.

(Psalm 97:1–2)

The psalmist reminds us of the beauty of God's Reign. He describes the earth and sea, fire, lightning, and the heavens—all contributing to the glory of God. This is a beautiful time of year in many places, when the breezes of fall come in with the colored leaves and the smells of autumn. It looks like the earth is truly rejoicing in the wonders of God. Take some time to enjoy the beauty of the world. Even if you live in the city, find a park where you can sit and watch the trees and the birds. Imagine that all of nature has voices with which to praise and thank God for his presence and his glory among his people.

Lord God, creator of all that is good and beautiful, I praise you for the wonder of the natural world that I will encounter this week.

▸ To go deeper: Read and pray "The Beauty of Creation" near Philippians 4:8–9 in the *CYB*.

Feeling Wimpy?

I can do all things through him who strengthens me.

(Philippians 4:13)

When Paul wrote to the Philippians, he was in prison. He did not know if he was going to die or not. Yet he believed he was going to get through the ordeal with God's help. What is amazing is Paul's belief that God had given him good times and bad, and that in both, Paul knew God would always been there for him. What a wonderful example for us to follow! When you are down, when things are not going well, when you feel abandoned, have faith that God is with you and will strengthen you to endure whatever you have to face.

Blessed Trinity, Father, Son, and Holy Spirit, strengthen me to know you are present with me, especially when I am lonely and despairing. Let me know that your strength is there for me.

▸ To go deeper: Read the introduction to the Letter to the Philippians in the *CYB*.

Thankfulness

Then Jesus asked, "Were not ten made clean? But the other nine, where are they?"

(Luke 17:17)

Jesus cured ten lepers, but only one came back to say thank you. And that leper was a foreigner. Needless to say, Jesus was disappointed in the nine who took their cure for granted. Jesus's words caution us not to take God's gifts for granted. One of God's greatest gifts to us is the caring people most of us have in our lives. How often do we take our parents, friends, teachers, and brothers and sisters for granted? We sometimes fall into a mode of entitlement and act like we deserve all the good things and good people we have around us. Expressing gratitude is a sign of spiritual maturity.

Make a list of the ten most important people in your life. Find a way to express genuine gratitude to them for being for you and with you.

▸ To go deeper: Read "Give Thanks at All Times!" near 1 Thessalonians 5:18 in the *CYB*.

Don't Be Ashamed

For I am not ashamed of the gospel; it is the power of God for salvation to everyone who has faith.

(Romans 1:16)

Sometimes we might feel timid about being Christian. People can make fun of us for what we believe. The Gospel challenges us to care for others, to be genuine, to avoid hypocrisy, to follow the commandments, and to respect all life. Your peers might challenge your belief in chastity and your commitment not to use drugs and alcohol. Your Christian values and actions can be a source of embarrassment to some. But as Saint Paul says, by our baptism we are empowered to stand up for the values of Jesus and be proud to be followers of Christ.

Christ, my Lord, strengthen me through your Spirit to stand up for the Gospel and to try to live it out each day, even when it is questioned by others or when others make fun of me.

▶ To go deeper: Read "The Many Meanings of *Gospel*" near Romans 1:16 in the *CYB*.

Evil Makes Me Feel Disgusted

There will be anguish and distress for everyone who does evil . . . but glory and honor and peace for everyone who does good.

(Romans 2:9–10)

Having a peaceful heart is the result of doing good deeds, of caring for others, of going the extra mile, of living the Gospel. When we do evil deeds, we do not feel good about ourselves. We are often anxious, nervous, and ashamed. Have you ever told one lie to cover up an earlier lie? That is the dangerous downward spiral of sin. Evil beckons us to hide the sinful deed with more sins because we don't want others to discover the bad things we've done. Evil leads to a quagmire of self-doubts and unhappiness—just as doing good leads to honor.

Jesus Christ, you came to earth to bring forgiveness to all. Empower me to not drown in evil but to ask for forgiveness, to begin again to do honorable deeds.

▸ To go deeper: Pray "Examination of Conscience" near Romans 2:1–4 in the *CYB*.

He's Not Heavy; He's My Brother

Bear one another's burdens, and in this way you will fulfill the law of Christ.

(Galatians 6:2)

Saint Paul asks the Galatians to do several things in this chapter, including dealing with one another in a "spirit of gentleness" (6:1) and carrying one another's burdens. It is easy to treat people with indifference or self-righteousness. To relate with a gentle spirit takes thought and sensitivity. It requires one to walk in the shoes of another, to know the other person's pain and frustration. What burdens are carried by people you know? problems at home? struggles in classes? athletic missteps? the death or sickness of a parent or friend? addiction? What can you do to help them carry their burden?

Blessed Trinity, empower me to be sensitive to the needs of others at school, at home, and at work. Enable me to help carry the burdens of others so that they will not feel so alone.

▸ To go deeper: Read "The Principle of *Imani*" near Galatians 6:9 in the *CYB*.

Servant Leader

> [Jesus] got up from the table, took off his outer robe, and tied a towel around himself. Then he poured water into a basin and began to wash the disciples' feet.
>
> (John 13:4–5)

Reality television shows sometimes seem to suggest that success comes through manipulative and self-centered leadership. When Jesus washed the feet of the disciples, he showed them that leaders who follow him need to serve the needs of others and that no task is too lowly for such a leader. Such a leader is called a servant leader. Servant leaders serve those they guide with their leadership skills. They treat all with respect and do not expect special treatment for themselves. Do you see examples of servant leadership in your parish and in your school? In what ways are you a servant leader?

Name people you see as servant leaders. How do they serve others? As a leader yourself, act today in a way that shows your servant leadership style.

▸ To go deeper: Read and meditate on John 13:1–17.

Saint Teresa of Ávila

> In him you also, when you had heard
> the word of truth, the gospel of your
> salvation, and had believed in him,
> were marked with the seal of the
> promised Holy Spirit.
>
> (Ephesians 1:13)

Saint Teresa lived in the sixteenth century. For most of her early life, she never felt close to God, and she neglected her prayer life even though she became a Carmelite nun. At age forty-one she recommitted herself to prayer, and was rewarded with profound mystical experiences. But she was also practical, and set out to reform religious life to focus more on real prayer, simplicity, and humility. Despite much criticism and resistance, her efforts were eventually successful. We are called to respond to the same Gospel that Teresa was. In what way does your life mirror the truth of the Gospel?

Holy Spirit, help me to experience God in prayer as Saint Teresa did. Help me encourage others to live the simple truths of the Gospel of Jesus Christ.

▸ To go deeper: Read "I Give God Thanks for You!" near Ephesians 1:15–23 in the *CYB*.

Church Versus Government

> "Is it lawful to pay taxes to the emperor, or not?" . . . Then [Jesus] said to them, "Give therefore to the emperor the things that are the emperor's, and to God the things that are God's."
>
> (Matthew 22:17–21)

The Pharisees questioned Jesus about paying taxes. Jesus made a good distinction by pointing to the face of the emperor on a coin. He seemed to be saying that we shouldn't confuse worldly governments with God's Kingdom. Today we may have questions about the requirements of the government versus the teachings of the Church. The Church teaches that we should follow the laws of our nation unless they come into conflict with the laws of God. Thus some actions are not against civil law but are against Church teaching: abortion, for example. How will you respond if faced with this conflict?

Come, Holy Spirit, and fill me with wisdom to know when a civil law goes against God's law, and in those times, give me the courage to follow the laws of the Church.

▸ To go deeper: Read "Jesus and Civil Disobedience" near Matthew 21:12–13 in the *CYB*.

Pestering God

"And will not God grant justice to his chosen ones who cry to him day and night? Will he delay long in helping them?"

(Luke 18:7)

Jesus tells a parable about an unjust judge who has no time for God or people, but who answers the pleas of a widow because she keeps pestering him and wears him down. Although whining to parents and teachers is not necessarily recommended, Jesus encourages us to keep bringing our needs before God. For what do we need to cry to God day and night? What major concerns do we have? Remember, if your prayers do not seem to be answered right away, do not lose heart (see Luke 18:1). God's response can come through people and events in ways we do not expect or recognize at first.

Come, Holy Spirit, and fill me with hope so that I will not give up on pestering God about the things that are important to me. Help me to see God's answer to my prayers in the events of my life.

▶ To go deeper: Read and pray "Unanswered Prayer" near Mark 11:24 in the *CYB*.

Saint Luke

Do your best to come to me soon, for Demas, in love with his present world, has deserted me and gone to Thessalonica; Crescens had gone to Galatia, Titus to Dalmatia. Only Luke is with me.

(2 Timothy 4:9–11)

Early tradition says that the Luke referred to in the above passage is the author of the Gospel of Luke. This Gospel is directed to the Gentiles (non-Jews). Luke himself was probably a Gentile convert to Christianity. He was so moved by his experience of Jesus and the early Church that he wanted to write down the stories about Jesus for others like himself. Luke was especially moved by the stories of Jesus's mercy and his compassion for the poor and outcast, so he emphasizes those aspects of Jesus's life and teaching. Many people are drawn to his Gospel for that reason.

Dear Jesus, allow me to be inspired by both Paul and Luke, who gave of themselves 100 percent in spreading the good news of God's love and mercy.

▸ To go deeper: Read the introduction to the Gospel According to Luke in the *CYB*.

Be Prepared

Be dressed for action and have your lamps lit.

(Luke 12:35)

Jesus is reminding people that they need to be alert to the coming of God in their lives. He says we must be ready for the unexpected. He speaks of opening the door as soon as the master knocks. These images refer to God entering and reentering our lives. We need to be ready. We need to be attentive. We need to recognize God as he comes through people and the events of our lives.

We dress differently for different occasions. When you hear "Be dressed for action" as a symbol for responding to God, what images come to mind?

Jesus Christ, I was clothed in your garment at baptism. Continue to dress me for action as I proclaim your goodness through my life's actions and words.

▸ To go deeper: Read Luke 12:35–48.

Don't Be a Scoffer!

Happy are those
   who do not follow the advice of
      the wicked,
or take the path that sinners tread,
   or sit in the seat of scoffers;
but their delight is in the law of the
   LORD.

(Psalm 1:1–2)

Today the psalmist might say: "Don't follow advice from people who make trouble for others," "Don't take the path of least resistance," or "Know the values of those you hang out with." Sometimes it is easy to get into a mentality where you don't want anyone telling you what is right. You scoff at smart kids; you make fun of faculty who are serious about helping you learn and grow. You think your parents are out of touch. Follow the psalmist's advice and focus on the "law of the LORD," the law of love that Christ proclaimed.

God, Father of us all, strengthen me to embrace the attitude of the psalmist with his positive view of life. Enable me to delight in your law, which Jesus taught in all its fullness.

▸ To go deeper: Read "Understanding the Psalms" near Psalm 3 in the *CYB*.

Inner Conflict

> I can will what is right, but I cannot
> do it. For I do not do the good I want,
> but the evil I do not want is what I do.
> (Romans 7:18–19)

We all have moments when we feel like Saint Paul. We make up our minds to do something good, but we end up not doing it, or worse still, doing something that causes harm. To do good actions consistently, we need to be focused, we need to hang around with people who will support us, and we need to pray for strength to stay on track. Think of some times when you lost focus and did not do the good you intended to do. How could you change your strategy for the future?

Name one good thing you are going to do today. What will support your doing it? What obstacles will you face in accomplishing the task? Pray for strength to follow through.

▸ To go deeper: Read "Our Inner Struggle" near Romans 7:14–25 in the *CYB*.

Shape Up

I . . . beg you to lead a life worthy of the calling to which you have been called, with all humility and gentleness, with patience, bearing with one another in love, making every effort to maintain the unity of the Spirit in the bond of peace.

(Ephesians 4:1–3)

Paul reminds us here to take the high road. He names the virtues he expects to see in the followers of Christ. As you think about humility, gentleness, patience, love, unity, and peace, which of those do you feel you are consciously integrating into your life? Which one do you struggle with the most? When is it hardest to be patient and loving?

Jesus, my brother and my Lord, give me the desire to practice the virtues with which I struggle. Strengthen me to not give up, but to keep focusing on the person I can become with your help.

▶ To go deeper: Read "Weave for Us a Garment" near Ephesians 4:1–6 in the *CYB*.

Gifts for Ministry

The gifts he gave were that some
would be apostles, some prophets,
some evangelists, some pastors and
teachers, to equip the saints for the
work of ministry, for building up the
body of Christ.

(Ephesians 4:11–12)

In this passage Saint Paul names some of the gifts people
have for doing ministry. Have you ever considered
whether you have a gift for ministry in the Church? You
might be good at singing or public reading and could be a
cantor or lector. Maybe you have a gift for leading the
community in prayer or helping people understand the
teachings of Christ. Maybe you are good at organizing
service projects. Maybe you are even called to serve as a
priest or as a religious sister or brother—something to
which every Catholic youth should give some thought.

*Name three of your gifts. How do you use them for the good of the
Body of Christ? Pray for openness in using your gifts in service of the
Church.*

▸ To go deeper: Read "Ministry in the Church" near Acts of
the Apostles, chapter 15 in the *CYB*.

Give Generously

Give to the Most High as he has given
    to you,
  and as generously as you can afford.
For the Lord is the one who repays
  and he will repay you sevenfold.

(Sirach 35:12–13)

Sometimes we are so focused on ourselves that we concentrate on saving money for a whole list of things we want: clothes, music, videos, jewelry, and so on. Because of the temptation toward self-absorption, we are often insensitive to the needs of others. We just don't see them. When we give of ourselves or our resources to others, we are acting as God wants us to act. Jolting ourselves from our own little world to see the needs of others is what is expected of a disciple of Christ. As Sirach tells us, when we give to others, we are giving to God and will be rewarded by God.

God most high, jolt me from my own little world and empower me to be your generous ambassador to those in need. I ask this in the name of Jesus, my friend and brother.

▸ To go deeper: Read "Giving the Best of the Best" near
  2 Chronicles 31:2–10 in the *CYB*.

Tiny Seeds

He said therefore, "What is the kingdom of God like? And to what should I compare it? It is like a mustard seed that someone took and sowed in the garden; it grew and became a tree, and the birds of the air made nests in its branches."

(Luke 13:18–19)

Jesus used many images to help people understand what the Kingdom of God was all about. All the images were dynamic and pointed toward growth. The mustard seed is tiny, but it will produce a tree. Many of the great movements in the Church started that way: someone's idea about how to serve God took off and grew and grew. Think of the Franciscans, the Dominicans, Teens Encounter Christ, Marriage Encounter, and many others. Perhaps you will have the opportunity to be part of some Christian movement that started small and grew to become a powerful force for God.

Jesus Christ, I received the gift of faith at baptism. Enable the seed of faith to grow in me as I strive to become a faithful disciple through the power of the Holy Spirit.

▸ To go deeper: Read "The Kingdom Is Like . . ." near Matthew 13:10–53 in the *CYB*.

Abba, Father

> When we cry, "Abba! Father!" it is that
> very Spirit bearing witness with our
> spirit that we are children of God, and
> if children, then heirs, heirs of God
> and joint heirs with Christ—if, in fact,
> we suffer with him so that we may
> also be glorified with him.
>
> (Romans 8:15–17)

Paul is making it clear to us that we are children of God,
just as Christ was God's Son. Because of Christ we can
call God "Abba," which is like saying "Papa." Christ,
through his death and Resurrection, made it possible for
each of us to have an intimate relationship with God and
to inherit all that Jesus inherited. How is your faith
enriched by knowing that you can call God Abba or Papa?
What does this say to you about Christ's love for you and
his desire to be your brother?

*Abba, Papa, Jesus Christ taught us that we are your children and
that you want us to have a close and intimate relationship with you.
Help us to remember this and to pray to you as a loving Father.*

▸ To go deeper: Pray "A Parent's Love" near Hosea 11:1–7 in
the *CYB*.

Who Is on Our Side?

> If God is for us, who is against us? He
> who did not withhold his own Son,
> but gave him up for all of us, will he
> not with him also give us everything
> else?
>
> (Romans 8:31–32)

We often get bogged down in day-to-day living and forget
the big picture. We need to become more conscious that
God is behind us in all we do, even when the going gets
tough. As Paul reminds us, God the Father gave us his
Son, the greatest gift of all. Because he did this, God
certainly is not going to withdraw lesser gifts. Until we put
on the mind of Christ and start trusting in our heavenly
Father as Jesus did, we are missing a treasure of insight
and energy, which we need to be true disciples. That is
easier said than done, of course, but it is the key to
becoming all that God wants us to be.

*Jesus Christ, we know you intercede with the Father for us. Enable
us to be more like you by thinking and acting like you. Send the
Holy Spirit to help us each day.*

▶ To go deeper: Pray "Hopeless and Hurting" near 2 Corinthians 4:16–18 in the *CYB*.

Saints Simon and Jude

> So then you are no longer strangers and aliens, but you are citizens with the saints and also members of the household of God, built upon the foundation of the apostles and prophets, with Christ Jesus himself as the cornerstone.
>
> (Ephesians 2:19–20)

Simon and Jude were among the twelve Apostles, and when we celebrate their feast, we are reminded of our connection to the past, the meaning it brings for the present, and the energy it gives for the future. We are Christians today because of the faith of the Apostles and the actions they took in the name of Christ. They formed the early Church, which was a community of believers empowered by the Holy Spirit. What does it mean to be part of the "household of God"? A household is a group of people who work together, who help out one another, who share talents, and who contribute to the whole. God's house has room for all!

Dear Jesus, you are the cornerstone of my faith. I want to be a contributing member of your household of faith, continuing the work started long ago by saints like Simon and Jude.

▸ To go deeper: Read "Faith Versus Good Works" near Ephesians 2:1–10 in the *CYB*.

Spiritual Friendship

> I thank my God every time I remember you, constantly praying with joy in every one of my prayers for all of you. . . . I am confident of this, that the one who began a good work among you will bring it to completion by the day of Jesus Christ.
>
> (Philippians 1:3–6)

Saint Paul wrote to the Philippians from prison. Notice how upbeat he is. While he was suffering in prison because he was a follower of Christ, he kept his spirits up by the friends he had in Christ. The friends we have who share our belief in Jesus Christ can keep us going in good times and in bad times. Reread the passage and think about it as if Paul is talking directly to you today. Who are the people who share your belief in the Gospel of Jesus Christ? Do you have a commitment to supporting them in living the faith? Why would Paul be confident that you will continue to do good works all your life?

Dear Jesus, help me find and support the kind of friends Saint Paul had—friends who share a belief in you and support one another in good times and in hard times.

▸ To go deeper: Read "Friendship" near Philippians 1:3–11 in the *CYB*.

Bonded

> Have we not all one father? Has not one God created us? Why then are we faithless to one another, profaning the covenant of our ancestors?
>
> (Malachi 2:10)

If we are bonded in one God, why is it so hard to get along with one another? Why do we discriminate against others? Why are we so hard on one another? Take a moment in prayer today to think about how connected we are to other people. Start by praying for a good friend. Then think of the people who are close to your friend and pray for them. Pick one of those people, think about who they are close to, and pray for those people. Just imagine the number of people we are connected to through just one relationship! We have the power to touch many people's lives.

Holy Spirit, you give us the power to bond with other people through love, compassion, and service. Help me to be a positive link in the people I connect together.

▸ To go deeper: Read "A Pure Offering to God" near Malachi 1:1–11 in the *CYB*.

Love the Living

> You spare all things, for they are
> yours, O Lord, you who love the
> living.
> For your immortal spirit is in all
> things.
> (Wisdom of Solomon 11:26—12:1)

God loves us very much and sees us as his people. God's Spirit is in all things. In an era when we have cyberspace at our fingertips and can communicate with people around the world via the Internet, it is easy to forget that the important connection between all of us is the living God. As we get reports back from our space exploration that there is a good chance that there are other earthlike planets in the galaxy, we are blown away. We are reminded that our God is not limited to our world and the things we know—he is God of all living things wherever there may be life in the universe.

Lord, you love all living things, having imbued your Spirit in them. I praise you for the wonder of everything that lives and has its being in you!

▶ To go deeper: Read "Words from a Father to His Son!" and "Words from a Mother to Her Daughter!" near Wisdom, chapter 12 in the *CYB*.

All Saints

Beloved, we are God's children now;
what we will be has not yet been
revealed. What we do know is this:
when he is revealed, we will be like
him, for we will see him as he is.

(1 John 3:2)

Sometimes we look at our ancestors to understand our
own family story. It helps us to understand who we are
and to take encouragement from our ancestors. The saints
are part of our family, too, and can have that same role for
us. These are people who lived out their faith in Christ as
we do. They were mostly ordinary people like us who
never imagined themselves as becoming extraordinary. On
the feast of All Saints, we honor every person who has
lived a holy life, whether they are an official saint or not.
We connect with those ancestors in faith who can give us
courage and hope in living as a Christian.

*If you haven't already done so, learn about the saint whose name you
share. Pray to that person when you need help of any kind.*

▶ To go deeper: Read "The Communion of Saints" near
  1 Thessalonians 4:13–18 in the *CYB*.

All Souls

In the eyes of the foolish they seemed
   to have died,
and their departure was thought to be
   a disaster,
and their going from us to be their
   destruction;
but they are at peace.
                    (Wisdom of Solomon 3:2–3)

On this day we remember those we love who have died.
Carl's dad died when Carl was ten years old. They used to
ride their bikes together to a nearby park, buy ice cream,
sit in the grass, and talk while they ate it. Every year on
November 2, no matter what the weather is like, Carl
visits that spot, talks to his dad, and prays for him and
with him. Some people go to the cemetery on this day and
put flowers on the graves of those they miss. It is good to
remember and honor the dead.

*Heavenly Father, we know that death is just a passing from this
world into the fullness of your glory. I pray for those who have passed
from this life with the confidence that I will see them in the next.*

▸ To go deeper: Read "Surviving Grief" near 2 Samuel
   18:33—19:8 in the *CYB*.

Saint Martin de Porres

> Why do you pass judgment on your brother or sister? Or you, why do you despise your brother or sister? For we will all stand before the judgment seat of God.
>
> (Romans 14:10)

Martin de Porres lived in Peru in the sixteenth century. The sin of racism was alive and well, and he, being of mixed race, was treated like a slave. His family lived in poverty because his Spanish father abandoned them after Martin was born. As an adult, Martin joined the Dominican order and lived the Beatitudes of Christ by caring for the sick, feeding the hungry, and comforting the sorrowful. He is a great model of forgiveness for what he endured at the hands of racists.

Come, Holy Spirit, and help me reach out to someone today who experiences some kind of discrimination. Even a smile and a kind word can go a long way.

▶ To go deeper: Read "Respecting Differences" near Romans 14:1–23 in the *CYB*.

Saint Charles Borromeo

For I will not venture to speak of anything except what Christ has accomplished through me.

(Romans 15:18)

Saint Charles was a bishop in Milan, Italy. His appointment as bishop was delayed because the Council of Trent needed his skill as a behind-the-scenes leader when serious disagreements occurred—something he could not offer if he were a bishop attending the council. Charles believed that if the people were to live a good life, they needed the good example of the clergy and bishops. He set a powerful example himself during the plague—which in many ways was like our AIDS epidemic today—by borrowing huge sums of money to feed those who were starving and minister to those who were dying.

Pray to Saint Charles whenever you find your plans delayed or taking another direction. Ask him to help you see the good you can do in whatever circumstances you find yourself.

▶ To go deeper: Read "AIDS—a Matter of Justice" near Psalm 82 in the *CYB*.

The Ultimate Goal

I press on toward the goal for the prize of the heavenly call of God in Christ Jesus. Let those of us then who are mature be of the same mind.

(Philippians 3:14–15)

Once again Saint Paul reminds us that we will only be effective as disciples if we keep our ultimate goal in mind. And what is our ultimate goal? It is to share the resurrected life with Jesus Christ by being faithful to God in this life. All our other life goals must contribute to this ultimate goal. What is it that you want to accomplish with your life? What goals do you have for yourself? How will you accomplish those goals in a way that contributes to your ultimate goal? Like Saint Paul, let us be aware of our ultimate goal and stay committed to it.

Jesus, my friend, thank you for making it possible to share eternal life with God. Help me to keep my eyes set on this ultimate goal and to always live in a way that shows I believe in it.

▶ To go deeper: Read "Commitment to Your Goal" near Philippians 3:13–16 in the *CYB*.

Sadness and Hope

For since we believe that Jesus died and rose again, even so, through Jesus, God will bring with him those who have died.

(1 Thessalonians 4:14)

Have you ever had someone close to you die? What a devastating experience it can be! As sad as it is and as great as the loss feels to us, just imagine if we didn't believe that the dead rise and continue to live with God, that there is life after death! Our life on this earth is but a small step in a lifetime that includes heaven. Losing someone we dearly love is one of the hardest things we have to endure in this life. Yet we can endure it with the knowledge and hope that they are already living in the presence of the Lord.

Heavenly Father, I pray for the people I love who have died. I trust them to your infinite love and am confident that they are watching over me until we meet in heaven.

▶ To go deeper: Read "Trusting the Grace of God" near Romans 5:1–11 in the *CYB*.

You Are Brave

Be strong, and let your heart take
courage,
all you who wait for the LORD.
(Psalm 31:24)

You may not think of yourself as brave or courageous.
Remember, though, that being courageous doesn't mean
that you have no fear but that you act despite your fear.
Some people live their whole lives without ever going
against the crowd out of fear of being different. And
some teens, tired of always being fearful, decide to do
what is right despite what some of their peers may think.
Who is more courageous? Who lives a more fulfilling life?
Who would you rather be?

*Write about three times when you have acted with courage. Then
write about a way you can show courage this week. Ask Mary or
your patron saint to help you carry this out.*

▸ To go deeper: Read "Courage" near Psalm 31 in the *CYB*.

Watch Over Me

> The LORD is my shepherd, I shall not
>   want.
>   He makes me lie down in green
>   pastures;
> he leads me beside still waters;
>   he restores my soul.
>
> (Psalm 23:1–3)

Sometimes you may feel all alone. At those times it would be so nice to have someone take care of you—to solve all your problems and to be a faithful friend no matter what you did or what others said about you. Guess what! You do have someone like that, and you even know it when you stop and think about it. Psalm 23 is a famous prayer of confidence in the God who is always there for us. Most people today may not identify with sheep, but we can identify with the feeling that God's loving care makes all the difference when things get difficult.

Pray Psalm 23 slowly and reflectively. Think about how each verse is true in your life. Consider memorizing this psalm so you can repeat it whenever you need reassurance of God's care.

▶ To go deeper: Read "The Good Shepherd Looks After Us!" near Psalm 23 in the *CYB*.

God Lives Here

Do you not know that you are God's temple and that God's Spirit dwells in you?

(1 Corinthians 3:16)

Think of the most beautiful church you've ever seen. It is cared for out of respect for God's house. In this verse Saint Paul reminds us that the Holy Spirit also lives in each one of us. You yourself are a temple for the Holy Spirit. In what kind of a temple do you want the Holy Spirit to dwell? Caring for our own temple includes getting proper rest, putting healthy food into it, not abusing it with drugs or alcohol, and giving it the healthy exercise it needs. Our bodies need the same loving and proper care as any great cathedral!

Come Holy Spirit, and help me to take good care of your dwelling place in me. Let me not give in to the temptations that harm and abuse my body, especially over the long term.

▸ To go deeper: Read "From the Bottom Up" near 1 Corinthians 3:10–17 in the *CYB*.

Saint Leo the Great

Remind them to be subject to rulers and authorities, to be obedient, to be ready for every good work, to speak evil of no one, to avoid quarreling, to be gentle, and to show every courtesy to everyone.

(Titus 3:1–2)

Saint Leo was a pope who lived in the early centuries of the Church. Elected in 440, he was a talented administrator who was equally gifted at spiritual leadership. He was the first pope to claim to be Peter's heir and to have supreme authority over all the Church. He also strongly defended the teaching that Jesus was both fully human and fully divine against a heresy that taught that Jesus was only divine. He even courageously met with Attila the Hun and convinced him not to ransack the city of Rome. Leo understood the everyday needs of the people and was famous for his preaching.

Saint Leo tried to live the advice Saint Paul wrote to Titus. Read it again thoughtfully and see which part you might improve on in your life. Pray to Saint Leo to help you.

▶ To go deeper: Read "The Priesthood and Christ's Sacrifice" near Hebrews 4:14—5:10 in the *CYB*.

Saint Martin of Tours

> "The kingdom of God is not coming with things that can be observed; nor will they say, 'Look, here it is!' or 'There it is.' For, in fact, the kingdom of God is among you."
>
> (Luke 17:20–21)

Saint Martin became a Christian at the age of eighteen. Even though his father was a military officer, Martin believed that Christians were not allowed to kill, and became a conscientious objector even though he was imprisoned for refusing to serve in the military. As a priest, then a bishop, he founded monasteries and churches in present-day France. Once, the story goes, he met a beggar who was freezing in the cold. Martin tore his own cloak in half to share it with the man. The story of his life was written down and became one of the first and most popular lives of the saints.

Look in your own closet. Share what you have with those who may be cold this winter. Like Martin, you will help bring the Kingdom of God among us.

▶ To go deeper: Read "Ministers of the New Covenant" near 2 Corinthians 3:1–11 in the *CYB*.

Saint Josephat

And this is love, that we walk according to his commandments; this is the commandment just as you have heard it from the beginning—you must walk in it.

(2 John 6)

This saint who was a bishop and martyr spent his life working for the unity of all Christians. He was a reform-minded bishop who brought order and proper procedure into his diocese. Josephat also helped bring the Eastern Church of the Slavic countries into union with the Western Church (Rome). Tragically, he was killed by Christians who were determined to keep that from happening. Today we Christians are still divided, with 64 percent Roman Catholic, 13 percent Eastern Churches, and 23 percent Protestant. What message does this give to the 71 percent of the world that is non-Christian?

Spirit of unity, I pray that all the churches who believe in Jesus Christ as Lord and Savior may someday be united again. Help me be an ambassador for Christian unity.

▸ To go deeper: Read "Unwelcome Guests" in 2 John in the *CYB*.

Saint Frances Xavier Cabrini

Beloved, you do faithfully whatever you do for the friends, even though they are strangers to you; they have testified to your love before the church.

(3 John 5–6)

In this Scripture passage, the author is encouraging a Christian leader to open his home to Christian workers who were passing through his city. This admonition is appropriate for the feast day of Saint Cabrini, otherwise known as Mother Cabrini. She opened her heart and her home to orphans and the needy. In the course of her life, this American saint founded sixty-seven institutions dedicated to caring for poor, sick, uneducated, and abandoned people. She died in Chicago of malaria in one of the hospitals she founded.

Jesus, friend of the poor, bless all those who provide shelter and housing to people who are in need. Help me to be generous in extending hospitality in your name to those who need it.

▸ To go deeper: Read "Supporting the Ministry of Others" in 3 John in the *CYB*.

I Want to Do Better

Have you sinned, my child? Do so no
more,
  but ask forgiveness for your past
  sins.

(Sirach 21:1)

It is human to fail. Sometimes we do things that are
wrong and sometimes we neglect to do the good things
we can and should do. How blessed we are that God is
willing to forgive us and help us do better. A good
spiritual practice to develop is to take a few minutes at the
end of each day to take a moral inventory. Where and how
were you your best self? Where and how did you fail to
do good or perhaps even commit sin? Be honest with
yourself, and ask for God's forgiveness and help in doing
better tomorrow.

*Holy Spirit, help me to be honest with myself when I have sinned
and need forgiveness. Let me not despair when I've sinned, but be
sorry and trust in God's forgiveness.*

▶ To go deeper: Read and pray "Examine Your Conscience"
  near Sirach, chapter 21 in the *CYB*.

Celebrate at Church and at Home

> After he had said this, he went on ahead, going up to Jerusalem.
>
> (Luke 19:28)

It was time for the religious festival of the Passover, and Jesus, always respecting the holy days of his religious tradition, went to Jerusalem to celebrate it. We, too, have special holy days: Holy Thursday, Good Friday, the Easter Vigil and Easter Sunday, Pentecost, Marian feasts, and saints' feasts throughout the year. Many people look forward to those feasts as opportunities to remember and celebrate all that God has done for us. Like Jesus, you can honor what you believe by celebrating your faith both at home and at church—around the family table and the altar table.

Talk with your parents about how you can celebrate your religion at home. Perhaps you can have special meals on your saints' feasts or other important feasts.

▸ To go deeper: Read "The Liturgical Year" near Luke 3:15–22 in the *CYB.*

Our Friend Is Waiting

> Zacchaeus stood there and said to the Lord, "Look, half of my possessions, Lord, I will give to the poor; and if I have defrauded anyone of anything, I will pay back four times as much."
>
> (Luke 19:8)

What an amazing promise Zacchaeus made! Though Jesus was criticized for befriending Zacchaeus, the sinner and assumed cheater, in his typical fashion, Jesus still reaches out to him. The same is true today. No matter how we fail and what others think of us, Christ is there to befriend us. Will we be as generous as Zacchaeus in our response? Will we be willing to make amends to anyone we've hurt or to repair or replace anything we've damaged? Taking those steps is difficult, but the integrity it gives us is irreplaceable.

Dear Jesus, you were so amazing in your response to those society had rejected. As I let you into my life, help me be as generous as Zacchaeus in making amends for my sins.

▶ To go deeper: Read "Noticed by Jesus" near Luke 19:1–10 in the *CYB*.

What's in Your Diet?

> Do not be conformed to this world,
> but be transformed by the renewing
> of your minds, so that you may
> discern what is the will of God—what
> is good and acceptable and perfect.
>
> (Romans 12:2)

What a challenge: not to be conformed to this world! We are immersed in it every day of our lives. God created a world good and gracious, but the messages that come to us every day in entertainment, news, and music, and from some media stars are not always consistent with the will of God. In many cases they are just the opposite. We must follow Paul's advice and analyze everything we see and hear by the values and teachings of Jesus and the Church. When you listen to a song or watch a movie or read an advertisement, always ask yourself, "Does watching or listening to or buying this product bring me closer to Jesus?"

Decide whether you will "fast and abstain" from certain movies, television programs, musicians, and so on because they feed you a diet of messages you do not want to buy into.

▸ To go deeper: Read "We Are the Body of Christ!" near Romans 12:1–8 in the *CYB*.

It's Yours to Spend

O give thanks to the LORD, for he is
    good;
  for his steadfast love endures
    forever.
. . . .
Let them extol him in the
    congregation of the people,
  and praise him in the assembly of
    the elders.

(Psalm 107:1,32)

If we had no other gift from God but the gifts of life and
love, we could spend our entire lifetime in a prayer of
thanks for these amazing gifts. Yet each of us has also
been entrusted with a personality, a set of talents, and the
freedom to choose how to use our life. There are two
ways to look at this. One is that it is a burden from which
to escape. Unfortunately many people see it that way. The
other way to see it is as the psalmist sees it, as wonderful
opportunities for which we must praise God. How will
you spend what God has given you?

*Heavenly Father, I praise you again for the gift of life and for your
steadfast love. Help me to be joyful and not feel burdened by the
freedom to choose, with which you bless us.*

▶ To go deeper: Read "Thankfulness" near Psalm 107 in the
  CYB.

Rose Philippine Duchesne

Rejoice always, pray without ceasing,
give thanks in all circumstances; for
this is the will of God in Christ Jesus
for you.

(1 Thessalonians 5:16–18)

Sister Rose Duchesne was known for praying without
ceasing. She was also a woman who gave thanks to God,
even though as a missionary to the United States, she
lived a life of great physical hardship on the frontier. Sister
Rose was a Frenchwoman who came to this country to
serve the Native Americans. She lived in Kansas and
Missouri. There the Native Americans called her "Woman
Who Prays Always."

*Native people in this country and in other parts of the world still
have many needs. Remember those people in your prayers and
whenever the opportunity to help arises.*

▸ To go deeper: Pray the "Iroquois Prayer of Thanksgiving"
near 1 Thessalonians 5:16–24 in the *CYB*.

The Easy Road

Do not follow your base desires,
  but restrain your appetites.

. . . .

Do not revel in great luxury,
  or you may become impoverished
    by its expense.

(Sirach 18:30–32)

It is usually much easier to give in to ourselves when we want something than it is to exercise self-control. And temptations are with us every day: to overeat, to overspend or overcharge, to be lazy, to use drugs or alcohol, and the list goes on and on. You think, if I have this new CD or DVD or these new clothes or this extra scoop of ice cream, I will be satisfied. And before you know it, you have become impoverished by giving in to the myth that something other than God will truly satisfy. Ben Sira, the wise man who wrote this book of the Bible, had it right.

Come, Holy Spirit, and fill my heart with the richness that comes from knowing God and doing God's will, rather than with the emptiness of accumulating material things.

▸ To go deeper: Read "Don't Get Burned" near Sirach 18:30—19:3 in the *CYB*.

The Presentation of the Blessed Virgin Mary

He said, "Truly I tell you, this poor widow has put in more than all of them; for all of them have contributed out of their abundance, but she out of her poverty has put in all she had to live on."

(Luke 21:3–4)

It was the custom in Mary's time that Jewish parents would take their young children to the temple to dedicate them to God. We assume that was true of Mary's parents, too, and that is the basis for today's feast day. We know that Mary, like the poor widow, gave all she had to God. She freely gave Jesus to the whole world. Through our vocational call, we also freely share Jesus with the world. Whether it is as a priest, a sister, a brother, or a married or single layperson, we are all called to have the generosity of the widow in sharing our time, talent, and treasure with others.

Spend a few minutes praying today to the Holy Spirit for guidance in discerning your vocational call. Through what vocation is God calling you to share Jesus with the world?

▸ To go deeper: Read "Prepare the Way" near Malachi 3:1–7 in the *CYB*.

Saint Cecilia

All their neighbors aided them with
silver vessels, with gold, with goods,
with animals, and with valuable gifts.

(Ezra 1:6)

Very little is known of Saint Cecilia. It is thought that she
was martyred for her faith. She is the patron saint of
musicians and is usually pictured with some kind of
musical instrument. Music is a valuable gift in our lives.
Even more than the gold or goods used by the priest Ezra
to rebuild the Temple, it has the power to uplift and
comfort, and to inspire. If you have musical ability, use it
to enrich your friends and family, people in a nursing
home, or your choir. There is also a saying, "Whoever
sings, prays twice." So whatever your singing ability may
be, sing at Mass—remember, you are praying twice!

*Thank you, God, for the birds that sing to us and for all people who
lift our hearts with their music.*

▶ To go deeper: Pray "Psalm 150, Part 2" near Psalm 150 in
the *CYB*.

We're All Hungry

"For the bread of God is that which comes down from heaven and gives life to the world." They said to him, "Sir, give us this bread always."

(John 6:33–34)

At different times we need different things to be fully alive. We always need food and the physical nourishment it provides. But we also need spiritual nourishment for fullness of life. We need such things as confidence and courage, comfort and peace, friendship and love. Jesus says to come to him with our needs. He offers us himself as the bread of life in the Eucharist, and he is there with so much more for us when we ask.

What kind of "bread" do you especially need to be fed with just now? Ask Jesus for that in your prayer tonight.

▶ To go deeper: Read "'I Am' Sayings of Jesus" near John 5:16–18 in the *CYB*.

Always Loyal

> Know therefore that the LORD your
> God is God, the faithful God who
> maintains covenant loyalty with those
> who love him and keep his command-
> ments, to a thousand generations.
> (Deuteronomy 7:9)

Such a loving God Moses describes here, whose faithful
love for us goes on for a thousand generations! Keep in
mind that in the Bible, the number *one thousand* often
symbolizes a number that is too big to count, so the Bible
is telling us that God's love for us goes on for countless
generations. All that is asked of us is that we love God
back. Friendships fade, marriages break up, and yesterday's heroes and heroines are forgotten today. But our
God never leaves us and never stops caring for us—no
matter what.

*Faithful God, your love for us knows no bounds. It is only because
of your love for me that I can be faithful in return, loving you and
keeping your commandments.*

▶ To go deeper: Read "The Shema: Putting God First" near
Deuteronomy 6:4–9 in the *CYB*.

Thanks Giving

And now bless the God of all,
who everywhere works great
wonders,
who fosters our growth from birth,
and deals with us according to his
mercy.

(Sirach 50:22)

Blessing God and being thankful are two of the most important attitudes of a Christian. Our most important prayer, the Eucharist, is a great prayer of thanksgiving to God for all the gifts we have received—which is why many churches have special masses on Thanksgiving Day. During this time of year, we are reminded to be thankful for all the material blessings we have. Even more important are the blessings that we cannot see or eat at a Thanksgiving feast. As a way of blessing God, thank someone who has been an important part of your life. Try to be as specific as possible.

Spend time today thinking about all you have been given without any effort on your part. Pray your own prayer of thanksgiving to God. Commit to blessing God regularly in your prayers.

▶ To go deeper: Read "Gratitude" near Psalm 116 in the *CYB*.

A Gift to Me

> He called the crowd with his disciples, and said to them, "If any want to become my followers, let them deny themselves and take up their cross and follow me."
>
> (Mark 8:34)

Throughout this Gospel, Mark shows us three qualities of discipleship. First, it is a gift to be called by God. Jesus called the first disciples, and he calls us. Discipleship is also a privilege, and a privilege is not to be taken for granted. This privilege needs to be fed and grown, and not kept in the box of what we thought about our faith as a child. Finally, Mark shows us that discipleship is all about following Jesus. How simple. How challenging. What things are you doing to keep your faith growing and maturing? How will you follow Jesus this week?

Thank you, Lord, for the gift and the privilege of being a disciple of Christ. Open my eyes to the unique way you are calling me to live out this gift.

▸ To go deeper: Read "Total Commitment" near Mark 8:34–38 in the *CYB*.

More Than This

> For this reason, those who believe are
> blessed with Abraham who believed.
> (Galatians 3:9)

As you grow older, you will probably experience an intense longing for something more in life. We try to fill this empty place in our hearts with relationships, activities, and often addictive behaviors. But it cannot be filled with those things. The longing in every human heart can only be filled by God. People may describe it in different ways: finding a purpose in life, hoping there's more than this world, wanting to belong to something bigger. You will truly be a wise person if you realize at your young age the folly of trying to fill this longing with anything other than your relationship with God.

Come, Holy Spirit, and fill my life with the love, joy, and peace that you alone can bring. Keep me from empty and even sinful attempts to fill the place in my heart that can only be filled by you.

▸ To go deeper: Read "Saved by Christ" near Galatians 3:1—4:7 in the *CYB*.

What Have I Said?

The centurion answered, "Lord, I am
not worthy to have you come under
my roof; but only speak the word, and
my servant will be healed."

(Matthew 8:8)

Do the words the centurion said so many centuries ago
sound familiar? They are the basis for the words we say at
Mass before Communion. Imagine if the words you said
yesterday would be repeated in public for generations. Is
there anything you would wish you hadn't said? The
words we say may not affect generations of people, but
they do impact those who are close to us. And once
something is said, we cannot take it back, and even our
regret and apologies cannot erase the sting of hurtful or
ill-chosen words.

*Lord, let the words I speak be worthy of the person you want me to
be. Especially when I'm tempted to speak unkind or harsh words,
help me to think before saying anything.*

▶ To go deeper: Read Matthew 8:5–13.

The Peaceable Kingdom

The wolf shall live with the lamb,
　　the leopard shall lie down with the
　　　　kid,
the calf and the lion and the fatling
　　　together,
　　and a little child shall lead them.

(Isaiah 11:6)

This chapter in Isaiah gives us the famous image of a peaceful place where animals that usually are enemies get along and even rest together. The peaceable kingdom, as it's called, has been the subject of paintings, poems, and essays. It endures because it is what our heart longs for. But as a human race, we all too often try to impose our will on others for personal gain, revenge, and the sheer high of being in control. The result is a never-ending spiral of violence. Jesus stands in opposition to all violence as he shows us the way to Isaiah's vision of the peaceable kingdom.

Take one action to be a peacemaker at home or among your friends. Learn about the Catholic teaching on just war, which justifies violence only as a last resort and only to stop a greater evil.

▶ To go deeper: Read "Lions and Lambs" near Isaiah 11:6–9 in the *CYB*.

Saint Andrew, Apostle

> As he walked by the Sea of Galilee, he
> saw two brothers, Simon, who is
> called Peter, and Andrew his brother,
> casting a net into the sea—for they
> were fishermen. And he said to them,
> "Follow me, and I will make you fish
> for people."
>
> (Matthew 4:18–19)

Matthew tells us that Andrew was a fisherman, along with
his brother Peter. In the Gospel of John, we learn that
Andrew was also a disciple of John the Baptist (see 1:40).
With John the Baptist, Andrew was waiting for the arrival
of the Messiah. And now here was Jesus, inviting Andrew
to follow him. Andrew's hope had come true. What are
your hopes and dreams? What would you hope to
accomplish in your life? Will you join Saint Andrew in
following Jesus Christ in fulfillment of your life's dream?

*Saint Andrew, help me to be as clear and certain in hearing the call
of Christ in my life as you were when Jesus called you.*

▶ To go deeper: Read "Follow Me" near Matthew 4:18–22 in
the *CYB*.

Hanging In There with God!

> Trust in the LORD forever,
>   for in the LORD GOD
>   you have an everlasting rock.
>
> (Isaiah 26:4)

In this verse from Isaiah, God is compared to a strong rock. This is a fitting image at a time when we are experiencing so much change. Technology is developing at such a high speed that it boggles the mind. People are losing their lives in conflicts that they didn't start or that are beyond their control. Corruption is found in many global institutions that were once thought trustworthy. You may wonder what you can contribute to a world that seems to be ever-changing. Amid those many changes, it is a blessing to know that the one thing we can count on is God, who is our anchor, our rock.

God, our rock, we know you are there for us. You are strong and ever-present. Be with us in these times of change. Strengthen and encourage us. We ask this in Jesus's name.

▸ To go deeper: Read "Get Close to God" near Genesis 18:22–23 in the *CYB*.

The Lord Is My Light!

The LORD is my light and my
   salvation;
      whom shall I fear?
The LORD is the stronghold of my
   life;
      of whom shall I be afraid?

(Psalm 27:1)

This psalm reminds us that we have nothing to fear because the Lord is always with us. The Lord enlightens our lives by showing us how to live, by comforting us when we are down, and by putting people in our lives to help us. The Lord gives us directions through the Scriptures, through the liturgy, and especially through people who help us interpret God's plans for us. Adults are often God's messengers to us. They care about us, and God comforts us through them. We in turn comfort others and become lights to them.

Think of people who have been God's messengers to you. Think of times when you have been a messenger of God to others. Thank God for the people in your life and the opportunities to help others.

▶ To go deeper: Read and pray Psalm 27, a triumphant song of confidence.

Saint Francis Xavier

It will be said on that day,
  Lo, this is our God; we have waited
    for him, so that he might save us.
  This is the LORD for whom we
    have waited;
  let us be glad and rejoice in his
    salvation.

(Isaiah 25:9)

Saint Francis Xavier was a Jesuit missionary to India and
Japan. He brought the message of Jesus to people who
had never heard of Christ. Because of Saint Francis
Xavier's efforts, there are Christians in India and Japan
today, although they are a small minority of the people.
Missionaries make great sacrifices when they go to foreign
countries. They have to learn the customs of the people,
which are different from their own. They have to build
trust with the people to prepare them to hear the word of
God. If you were a missionary to another country, what
would be the hardest adjustment for you?

*Lord Jesus, give me the courage to consider how I might spread your
word as Saint Francis Xavier did. Help me to endure any hardships
I might experience in spreading your word through my actions today.*

▶ To go deeper: Read "Preference for the Poor" near Isaiah
  29:17–21 in the *CYB*.

Prepare!

"See, I am sending my messenger
    ahead of you,
  who will prepare your way;
the voice of one crying out in the
    wilderness:
  'Prepare the way of the Lord,
  make his paths straight.'"

(Mark 1:2–3)

The cousin of Jesus, known as John the Baptist, was sent by God to prepare the people to receive Jesus. John preached repentance, which basically means to have a change of heart so that we may embrace the way God wants us to live. Advent is a good time to think about how our hearts might be changed to reflect the presence of Jesus Christ to a greater degree. How prepared is your heart to embrace the values of Jesus, especially as lived in the Church? What places in your heart have you kept closed to change? Open your heart fully to prepare yourself for the coming of Christ at Christmas.

God, you gave us Jesus to show us that you love us and as an example of how to be filled with love ourselves. Help me to open my heart to your love in preparation for Jesus coming anew at Christmas.

▸ To go deeper: Read the introduction to the Gospel According to Mark in the *CYB*.

Blind to God's Presence

The blind men came to him; and Jesus said to them, "Do you believe that I am able to do this?" They said to him, "Yes, Lord." Then he touched their eyes and said, "According to your faith let it be done to you."

(Matthew 9:28–29)

Oftentimes miracles in the Scriptures are connected to faith. Jesus uses the miracle to draw attention to the faith of the people. Today we are called to see with the eyes of faith. Faith helps us see the needs of others; faith helps us make sense of our lives and see how all the pieces fit together; faith helps us see God acting in ways that others overlook; faith gives us patience to keep looking for our path even when we can't see where God is leading us; faith helps us see that we are loved and valued in the eyes of God.

Dear Jesus, you helped the blind to see because they believed in you. Fill me with faith to see you acting in my life and the lives of others, especially during this Advent season.

▸ To go deeper: Read "Miracles and the Reign of God" near Matthew 8:1—9:34 in the *CYB*.

Saint Nicholas

"What do you think? If a shepherd
has a hundred sheep, and one of them
has gone astray, does he not leave the
ninety-nine on the mountains and go
in search of the one that went astray?"
(Matthew 18:12)

Saint Nicholas was a bishop, and bishops are often
referred to as the shepherds of the people of God in the
Church. Accounts credit Saint Nicholas with saving the
lives of three daughters who were destined for prostitu-
tion because their father could not supply their dowries—
the marriage gift to the groom's family. Saint Nicholas
supposedly left three bags of gold in the middle of the
night, thereby rescuing the daughters from a life of sin.
This legend led to Saint Nicholas being named the patron
saint of children, and it includes the custom of giving
treats to children in honor of his feast day.

*Think of ways to give surprise treats to your friends and family on
Saint Nicholas day, as a way of reminding them that they are special
and that you care about them. Thank God for those who care for you.*

▸ To go deeper: Read "Santo Nino" near Matthew 18:1–11 in
the *CYB*.

Love, Knowledge, and Insight

> And this is my prayer, that your love may overflow more and more with knowledge and full insight to help you to determine what is best, so that in the day of Christ you may be pure and blameless.
>
> (Philippians 1:9–10)

In preparing for the celebration of Christmas, we are challenged to discern what is best for us in our lives. "Best for us" means best not in a selfish or self-centered way, but best in terms of what Christ expects of us and how well we are contributing to the Kingdom of God. It is not always easy to know what Christ wants of us. We need, as Saint Paul says, more knowledge and insight to be in tune with Christ. This happens through prayer. That is why during Advent, the Church calls us to slow down, take time to be quiet, and reflect on the Scriptures.

Dear Jesus, these are busy days. I have a lot to do to get ready for Christmas. Help me to take quiet time to reflect on what is important this season—giving to others in your name.

▶ To go deeper: Read the introduction to the Letter to the Philippians in the *CYB*.

Immaculate Conception

"Greetings, favored one! The Lord is with you."

(Luke 1:28)

Mary, under the title of the Immaculate Conception, is the patroness of the United States, so December 8 is a special feast for us. The Gospel citation above is part of the story of the Annunciation. When you hear this read during Mass, you need to know that God is also talking to you. Like Mary, you are also God's favored ones. God is with us today. What does that mean? As you prepare to celebrate Christmas, the great feast of God-with-us, remember that this favor includes a responsibility to bring Christ to others, just as Mary did. Let Mary inspire you to be faithful in answering God's call.

"Hail Mary, full of grace, the Lord is with you. Blessed are you among women, and blessed is the fruit of your womb, Jesus."

▶ To go deeper: Read "Hail Mary" near Deuteronomy 28:1–6 in the *CYB*.

God Comforts Us

Comfort, O comfort my people,
    says your God.
Speak tenderly to Jerusalem,
    and cry to her.

(Isaiah 40:1–2)

This passage from Isaiah is referring to the Babylonian exile of the Jews, that terrible time when the Jewish nation was destroyed and all the leaders taken into captivity. Isaiah uses the word *Jerusalem* to refer to the Jewish community. These words are also meant for us today. Think of them being spoken to the people of New York after 9-11. Reflect on them being proclaimed to you at the present moment. What comfort do you need at this time? How can you comfort others? How can you speak tenderly to others?

Dear God, I need to be comforted about all that frustrates me and causes me to lose hope. I need comfort because of my own weakness. Empower me to reach out to others and comfort them.

▸ To go deeper: Read "The Hope of Second Isaiah" near Isaiah 40:1–5 in the *CYB*.

Where Have You Been?

Have you not known? Have you not
    heard?
The LORD is the everlasting God,
    the Creator of the ends of the
        earth.
He does not faint or grow weary.

(Isaiah 40:28)

In a throwaway world, a world where it seems everything is constantly in need of upgrades to stay current, it is comforting to know that God is everlasting. God does not need improving. God does not tire. He does not give up on us. He is always there for us. God, through us, is constantly recreating the world. God is empowering us to learn more, to be creative, and to care for all creation. To do that, we need to be in tune with God and appreciate his presence in our lives.

God, our creator, help me to know you better and to appreciate that your love never is out of date. Challenge and support me as I assist in the work of building your Kingdom on earth.

▶ To go deeper: Read "Between a Rock and a Soft Place" near Isaiah 40:1–11 in the *CYB*.

The Spirit of the Lord

> The spirit of the Lord GOD is upon
> me,
>> because the LORD has anointed me;
> he has sent me to bring good news to
> the oppressed,
>> to bind up the brokenhearted,
> to proclaim liberty to the captives,
>> and release to the prisoners.
>> (Isaiah 61:1)

These words from Isaiah were first spoken more than five hundred years before Christ was born. Later, in Luke's Gospel, Jesus applies them to himself. Today we hear them being applied to ourselves. The Holy Spirit is given to us at baptism. We are anointed to share in the life of Christ. Confirmation intensifies that life in us. God anoints us to bring good news to others, to heal the brokenhearted, and to free people from sin and injustice. What good news do you have to share with others? How can you help others live more freely? How can you help heal the brokenhearted?

Dear Jesus, we can easily forget the mission to which you call us. Help us to realize that your Spirit is with us to spread good news to others.

▶ To go deeper: Read Isaiah 61:1–11.

Our Lady of Guadalupe

"Blessed are you among women, and
blessed is the fruit of your womb. And
why has this happened to me, that the
mother of my Lord comes to me?"
(Luke 1:42–43)

A Mexican Indian boy, Juan Diego, was going about his
daily business when Our Lady appeared to him on several
occasions and asked him to tell the bishop that she wished
to have a church built in her honor. The bishop, however,
refused to believe Juan Diego. As a sign of the truth of his
story, Our Lady had Juan gather a bunch of roses in his
cloak to take to the bishop. When Juan unwrapped his
cloak, not only were there roses but also an imprint of
what we now know as Our Lady of Guadalupe. Mary is a
source of help for all people today. She is a symbol of the
goodness that can come out of suffering and difficulty.

*"Holy Mary, mother of God, pray for us sinners, now and at the
time of our death. Amen."*

▸ To go deeper: Read "Our Mother of Guadalupe, a Gift from
God!" near John 19:25–27 in the *CYB*.

Saint Lucy

At that time I will change the speech
    of the peoples
  to a pure speech,
that all of them may call on the name
    of the LORD
  and serve him with one accord.

(Zephaniah 3:9)

Saint Lucy is a beloved saint in Rome and Sicily. She died a martyr around the year 304. She gave herself totally to Christ in all things. The reading for her feast points to pure speech and service to the Lord. All of us can clean up our language and be more careful of how we talk with one another. Avoiding vulgar language is one way to show respect for others, and it certainly leads others to see us as people who call on the name of the Lord and serve the Lord with our whole being. During Advent, make a concerted effort to be a person of pure speech.

Make a list of slang or vulgar expressions that you use regularly. Find more appropriate words that show greater maturity and respect for others. Pray for God's strength to use those words instead.

▸ To go deeper: Read "Material Poverty and Spiritual Poverty!" near Zephaniah 3:11–13 in the *CYB*.

Saint John of the Cross

Turn to me and be saved,
   all the ends of the earth!
For I am God, and there is no other.
(Isaiah 45:22)

Saint John of the Cross, a sixteenth-century mystic, was
responsible for reforming the Carmelite Order. He was a
person who lived an austere life, renouncing many of the
things of the world. John was a man of intense prayer who
often prayed to Jesus as his savior and had great dedica-
tion to the cross of Christ. He would have been familiar
with the above passage from Isaiah. Today we need to be
saved from the materialistic values of the world. We are
bombarded with "things"—things we want for ourselves,
things we want to buy for others. How can you simplify
your life as you prepare to celebrate Christmas?

*Lord Jesus, empower us to simplify our lives as John of the Cross
did. Strengthen us to remember poor people at this time of year and
to use our resources to bring joy to their lives.*

▶ To go deeper: Read "I Will Never Forget You, My People"
   near Isaiah 49:13–16 in the *CYB*.

Healed by God

> O LORD my God, I cried to you for
>   help,
>   and you have healed me.
>
> (Psalm 30:2)

Sometimes we need to be healed from a disease. Sometimes we suffer from a wounded ego. At other times we feel depressed and lonely. David, the psalmist, reminds us that God can heal us from all that hurts us. Advent is a time to focus on all the good that God has done, and will continue doing, for us. When have you felt in need of healing? Of what do you need to be healed? Quiet yourself and let God heal your spirit of all the troubles you are carrying.

Dear God, heal me of the worries in my life. Help me to forgive myself for not accomplishing everything I set out to do. Strengthen me, and let me feel your presence when I feel down or lonely.

▸ To go deeper: Read and pray Psalm 30.

Be Just!

Thus says the LORD:
   Maintain justice, and do what is
      right.

(Isaiah 56:1)

God's command to be a just person is challenging. Often we are tempted to boast about ourselves when others should be getting the credit. Sometimes we hoard things for ourselves instead of sharing with others. At other times we forget about poor, lonely, and deprived people, and focus totally on ourselves. Isaiah tells us that from God's perspective, working for justice isn't just a nice thing to do, it is our moral obligation. In our hearts we know we must work for a just world. During this time of preparing for the celebration of Christmas, what can you do to act justly?

Pray and reflect on justice issues in your school or community. Decide on one thing you can do before Christmas that will promote a more just society.

▸ To go deeper: Read "God Wants Justice, Not Empty Rites!" near Isaiah 1:10–20 in the *CYB*.

O Wisdom

The spirit of the LORD shall rest on
   him,
      the spirit of wisdom and under
         standing.

(Isaiah 11:2)

For the next seven days, the prayer that ends each
reflection will be the O Antiphon for that day. The O
Antiphons are the Churchs' prayers during Advent that
highlight the different titles given to the Messiah in the
Book of Isaiah. Today's antiphon, "O Wisdom," mentions
God's tender care for all creation. Consider how you can
make wise decisions about using the earth's resources.
How can you contribute to a future that wisely promotes
the sustainable use of natural resources? Can your family
and friends make a plan to reduce or recycle items as part
of your Christmas gift exchange?

*"O Wisdom, O holy Word of God, you govern all creation with
your strong yet tender care. Come and show your people the way to
salvation."*

▸ To go deeper: Read "Wisdom Speaks" near Wisdom of
   Solomon, chapter 6 in the *CYB*.

O Sacred Lord of Ancient Israel

But there the LORD in majesty will be
   for us
   a place of broad rivers and streams.

· · · · · · · · · · · · · · · · · · ·

For the LORD is our judge, the LORD
   is our ruler,
   the LORD is our king; he will save
      us.

(Isaiah 33:21–22)

The "O Sacred Lord" antiphon reminds us that as our divine king, God is also a lawgiver. God gave Moses the Mosaic Law, which is summarized in the Ten Commandments. Yet in a mysterious way, God's law also makes us freer people. Have you ever considered that following the Ten Commandments actually frees us to do the works of mercy and justice–feeding the hungry, clothing the naked, giving drink to the thirsty, and so on? Sin makes us self-absorbed; living morally frees us to think of others. During this Advent make a renewed commitment to following God's law.

"O sacred Lord of ancient Israel, who showed yourself to Moses in the burning bush, who gave him the holy law on Sinai mountain: come, stretch out your mighty hand to set us free."

▶ To go deeper: Read "Advent Rejoicing" near Isaiah 35:1–10 in the *CYB*.

O Flower of Jesse's Stem

A shoot shall come out from the
stump of Jesse,
and a branch shall grow out of his
roots.

(Isaiah 11:1)

Jesse was King David's father. Micah, another Old Testament prophet, predicted that the Messiah would come from David's family tree. Remember that Mary and Joseph had to go to Bethlehem, the city of David's birth, to register right before Jesus was born. Today's O Antiphon recognizes that despite the fact that Jesus was a descendant of the greatest Jewish king, he is still a sign of salvation for all peoples. Think about your own ancestors. How have they influenced your faith? How have they helped you recognize Jesus as the Messiah?

"O Flower of Jesse's stem, you have been raised up as a sign for all peoples; kings stand silent in your presence; the nations bow down in worship before you. Come, let nothing keep you from coming to our aid."

▶ To go deeper: Read "Honoring Our Parents in God's Way!" near Sirach 3:1–16 in the *CYB*.

O Key of David

I will place on his shoulder the key of
the house of David; he shall open, and
no one shall shut; he shall shut, and
no one shall open.

(Isaiah 22:22)

Isaiah reminds us of the power of the Messiah to lead
people to God. The O Antiphon describes a Messiah of
great power—powerful enough to destroy death. Jesus,
the key of David, leads us out of the darkness of death
and oppression. Jesus Christ, the Messiah, by his life,
death and Resurrection, sets the direction for all of us. He
leads the way to a just and peaceful world. In what ways
would people describe you as just and peaceful? What
actions of justice and peace do you do regularly?

*"O Key of David, O royal Power of Israel controlling at your will
the gate of heaven: come, break down the prison walls of death for
those who dwell in darkness and the shadow of death; and lead your
captive people into freedom."*

▸ To go deeper: Read "Faith and Politics" near Isaiah 22:15–25
in the *CYB*.

O Radiant Dawn

The people who walked in darkness
  have seen a great light;
those who lived in a land of deep
  darkness—
    on them light has shined.

(Isaiah 9:2)

December 21 is the winter solstice, the day that has the least amount of light during the year in the northern hemisphere. To pray for "radiant light," the light of Christ, is very appropriate. The Israelites anticipated that the long-awaited Messiah would bring light to their lives and get rid of the gloom and oppression from which they had been suffering. Reflect on the lights you see at Christmastime. Which are your favorites? Why? How do they remind you of the "light of Christ"? How are you light to others? Who reflects Christ's light to you?

"O Radiant Dawn, splendor of eternal light, sun of justice: come, shine on those who dwell in darkness and the shadow of death."

▶ To go deeper: Read and pray "Christmas Light" near Isaiah 9:2–7 in the *CYB*.

O King of All the Nations

For a child has been born for us,
  a son given to us;
authority rests upon his shoulders;
  and he is named
Wonderful Counselor, Mighty God,
  Everlasting Father, Prince of Peace.
(Isaiah 9:6)

The many titles Isaiah attributed to the Messiah have been immortalized in music throughout the ages. All of them point to the Messiah being kind and compassionate as well as a ruler of nations. Choose a phrase that appeals to you from the above Scripture passage and reflect on it. What in the passage particularly speaks to you? How do you see Christ reflected in the passage?

"O King of all the nations, the only joy of every human heart; O Keystone of the mighty arch of humankind, come and save the creature you fashioned from the dust."

▶ To go deeper: Read and pray Isaiah 9:1–7.

O Emmanuel

> Therefore the Lord himself will give you a sign. Look, the young woman is with child and shall bear a son, and shall name him Immanuel.
>
> (Isaiah 7:14)

Remember that *Immanuel* (or *Emmanuel*) means "God with us." The O Antiphons culminate in the prophecy of the birth of Jesus. Isaiah foretold the coming of the Messiah about five hundred years before Jesus was born. At Christmas we pray that Christ comes anew into our hearts and lives. We know Christ is with us, but we want to continually grow in our appreciation and in our likeness of Christ. Throughout the Christmas liturgies, we ask to be renewed so that we can act more like Christ and make a significant difference in the world.

"O Emmanuel, king and lawgiver, desire of the nations, Savior of all people, come and set us free, Lord our God."

▶ To go deeper: Read "God-with-Us!" near Isaiah, chapter 7 in the *CYB*.

David, King and Servant

> I have found my servant David;
>   with my holy oil I have anointed
>   him;
> my hand shall always remain with him;
> my arm also shall strengthen him.
>
> (Psalm 89:20–21)

Jesus was a descendant of David. To prepare the people to be able to recognize Jesus as the Son of God, God called David and anointed him king of Israel. David reigned around the year 1000 BC. David tried to be faithful to God and God's mission, but at times he seriously sinned. However, he was not paralyzed by his sin. He asked for forgiveness and began again and again to faithfully serve God. David believed that God had placed great trust in him in choosing him to carry out his mission as king. David is your spiritual ancestor just as he was Jesus's ancestor. Follow in the footsteps of David and Jesus!

On this holy night, Lord Jesus, renew in us a desire to carry out your mission in the world, a world that is fractured with violence, hatred, and corruption. Enable us to be your peacemakers.

▶ To go deeper: Read "Jesus' Family Tree" near Matthew 1:1–17 in the *CYB*.

Christmas

"I am bringing you good news of great joy for all the people: to you is born this day in the city of David a Savior, who is the Messiah, the Lord."

(Luke 2:10–11)

The gift of Jesus is the greatest gift any of us could ever receive. God gave his very self to us in Jesus Christ. He loves us so much that he does not abandon us when we sin and stray from him. Just the opposite; he took the ultimate step of becoming one of us so that we could never doubt his love and care. God wants to give us the best he has, to show us how to be happy and how to create a better world. That is what we celebrate when we celebrate Christmas—God with us. So throughout this Christmas Day, remind yourself, "God is with us!"

God, our Father, our hearts are happy when we think of the wonderful gift you have given us in Jesus the Christ. As we celebrate Jesus's birth, I commit myself to striving to be more like him.

▸ To go deeper: Read "Jesus' Birth: Good News to the Poor" near Luke 2:8–20 in the *CYB*.

Saint Stephen

Stephen, full of grace and power, did great wonders and signs among the people. Then some of those who belonged to the synagogue . . . stood up and argued with Stephen. . . . They stirred up the people as well as the elders. . . . They dragged him out of the city and began to stone him.

(Acts of the Apostles 6:8–12, 7:58)

Stephen was the first Christian martyr. He believed in Jesus and preached in his name. But some of the Jewish leaders at the time were jealous and afraid of him, and ultimately stoned him to death. He died praying, "Lord Jesus, receive my spirit." Then he asked forgiveness for those who were killing him. Stephen was young and zealous in his efforts to follow Jesus. He made sacrifices. He was not swayed by the crowd but stood up and was counted for his beliefs. When have you had to defend your faith and stand up for what you believe? When have you had to stand alone and put your beliefs into practice?

Holy Spirit, give me courage to be a faithful witness like Stephen. Empower me to stand up and be counted when my beliefs are called into question and to live my life standing up for others.

▶ To go deeper: Read "Martyrs" near Acts, chapter 7 in the CYB.

Saint John the Evangelist

Light dawns for the righteous,
and joy for the upright in heart.
Rejoice in the LORD, O you righteous,
and give thanks to his holy name!
(Psalm 97:11–12)

Saint John was the author of the fourth Gospel, the last to be written. He was a mystic and very aware of the power of symbols. In fact, you will see the important symbols of light and darkness woven throughout his Gospel. The Christmas season is a season of light and joy. Reflect on the light and joy you bring to others during the holidays. What light and joy do they bring to you? Jesus said in John's Gospel, "I am the light of the world" (8:12). How has Jesus been light to you? He also said that "whoever follows me will never walk in darkness but will have the light of life" (8:12). What does the "light of life" mean to you?

Christ, my light, give me the vision to see you in the difficult times of my life. Enable me to be a light to others and to inspire them to follow you as Saint John did.

▶ To go deeper: Read "Jesus Is the Light of Life!" near John 8:12–59 in the *CYB*.

Holy Innocents

When Herod saw that he had been tricked by the wise men, he was infuriated, and he sent and killed all the children in and around Bethlehem who were two years old or under.

(Matthew 2:16)

The story of Herod murdering the children is just one of many stories of various government or religious officials being threatened by the thought of the Messiah. Their jealousy over Jesus's unofficial power and authority was a constant source of tension throughout Jesus's life. It ultimately caused his death on the cross. When do we feel most threatened by someone else? Is it because we perceive them to be better than we are? Is it because they are more popular than we are? What is the root cause of our feeling threatened? How can we overcome the feeling of being threatened by others?

Jesus, help me to relax and take a larger perspective when I feel threatened. Enable me to develop a cooperative spirit with those who seem vulnerable. Never let me use power for my own glory.

▶ To go deeper: Read "The Slaughter of the Innocents" near Matthew 2:16–18 in the *CYB*.

A Light for the Gentiles

> "Master, now you are dismissing your
> servant in peace,
> according to your word;
> for my eyes have seen your salvation,
> which you have prepared in the
> presence of all peoples,
> a light for revelation to the Gentiles."
>
> (Luke 2:29–32)

We take it for granted that Jesus is the savior of the whole human race. But in the early years of the Church, that was not commonly accepted. Thus the writer of Luke's Gospel goes to great lengths to show that Jesus came for all people, not just the house of Israel. For example, in this story of Jesus being presented in the Temple, the elderly Simeon recognizes that Jesus is the "light of revelation to the Gentiles." The majority of the world's population still does not recognize Jesus as the savior. As Christians we respect their beliefs, but we also pray for them to know the fullness of life and salvation that comes from knowing Jesus.

Among the people you know, who doesn't believe in Jesus as the savior? Make a habit of praying that all people will know the fullness of God's love through his Son, Jesus.

▸ To go deeper: Read Luke 2:22–38.

The Holy Family

Listen to me your father, O children;
  act accordingly, that you may be
    kept in safety.
For the Lord honors a father above
  his children,
    and he confirms a mother's right
      over her children.

(Sirach 3:1–2)

We celebrate the feast of the Holy Family (celebrated on the Sunday after Christmas) by reflecting on our own family. Notice how Sirach says that we are to be attentive to our parents for our own safety. It is a parent's job to worry about your safety—which they do a lot once you start driving a car and going out on your own with friends! Honoring your parents or guardians by communicating honestly with them contributes to a healthy family. Letting them know where you are and what you are doing contributes to their peace of mind. What other ways do you show love and respect for your parents and family?

Dear Jesus, besides getting lost as a boy, you must have experienced some conflicts with your parents. Enable me to work with my parents as you did with yours in an appropriate and peaceful way.

▶ To go deeper: Read "The Christian Family" near Colossians 3:18—4:1 in the *CYB*.

Get Ready for a New Year!

And the Word became flesh and lived among us, and we have seen his glory, the glory as of a father's only son, full of grace and truth.

(John 1:14)

We have lived another year in which we have been challenged to reflect on the mystery of the Incarnation—the Word becoming flesh and living among us. The fact that God became a human being makes all the difference in the world. God gave us Jesus to show us how to live, how to struggle, how to love. As we prepare for a new year, we need to think about how our lives must be different given this fact. In what ways are you Christ for others? How are others Christ for you? How can you help make the world a better place for all people?

Think of your New Year's resolutions in light of God becoming a human being. How will that belief influence your plans for the new year? Pray for the perseverance to live out your commitments.

▸ To go deeper: Read "Dying for New Life" near John 12:24–26 in the *CYB*.

ACKNOWLEDGMENTS

The scriptural quotation on April 12 is from the New Jerusalem Bible. Copyright © 1985 by Darton, Longman and Todd, London, and Doubleday, a division of Bantam Doubleday Dell Publishing Group, New York. All rights reserved.

All other scriptural passages contained herein are from the New Revised Standard Version of the Bible, Catholic Edition (NRSV). Copyright © 1993 and 1989 by the Di-vision of Christian Education of the National Council of the Churches of Christ in the United States of America. All rights reserved. Used with permission.

The prayer on July 31 is adapted from *The Spiritual Exercises of St. Ignatius: A Literal Translation and A Contemporary Reading*, Exercise no. 234, by David L. Fleming (Saint Louis: The Institute of Jesuit Sources, 1978), page 141. Copyright © 1978 by The Institute of Jesuit Sources. All rights reserved. Used with permission.

The prayers on December 8 and 12 are from *Catholic Household Blessings and Prayers*. Copyright © 1988 United States Conference of Catholic Bishops, Inc., Washington, DC. All rights reserved. Used with permission.

INDEX TO BIBLE VERSES

This index lists all the Bible verses used at the beginning of the reflections. They are arranged in the order that the books appear in the Bible. The abbreviations are the abbreviations used for the New American Bible translation.

Verse Used	Date	Verse Used	Date
Is 49:4	July 16	Mt 5:23–24	June 9
Is 49:5	May 14	Mt 5:37	June 11
Is 55:10	Mar 2	Mt 5:43–45	Mar 6
Is 55:11	July 10	Mt 6:2	Feb 25
Is 56:1	Dec 16	Mt 6:24	June 18
Is 61:1	Dec 11	Mt 7:7	Feb 17
Jer 1:5–7	July 21	Mt 7:12	June 21
Jer 1:7–8	June 23	Mt 7:15	June 17
Jer 3:15	July 23	Mt 7:17–20	June 22
Jer 17:7–8	Feb 24	Mt 8:8	Nov 28
Jer 20:13	Mar 18	Mt 8:13	June 25
Jer 31:1–3	Aug 3	Mt 9:6–7	July 1
Jer 31:33	Aug 5	Mt 9:9	July 2
Ez 16:59–60	Aug 13	Mt 9:9	Sept 21
Ez 18:23	Feb 18	Mt 9:28–29	Dec 5
Hos 6:1–3	Mar 5	Mt 9:37–38	July 5
Hos 10:12	July 7	Mt 9:37–38	June 12
Hos 11:1–3	July 8	Mt 10:40–42	July 11
Hos 14:9	Mar 4	Mt 10:42	June 26
Jon 1:2–3	Feb 16	Mt 11:28	June 3
Mi 6:8	July 19	Mt 11:29–30	July 15
Zep 3:9	Dec 13	Mt 13:8–9	July 20
Mal 2:10	Oct 30	Mt 13:54–55	July 30
Mt 2:16	Dec 28	Mt 16:15–16	Aug 4
Mt 2:11	Jan 6	Mt 16:24	Aug 28
Mt 2:14–15	Mar 19	Mt 17:7–8	Feb 20
Mt 4:18–19	Nov 30	Mt 18:12	Dec 6
Mt 5:3–9	June 6	Mt 18:20	Aug 11
Mt 5:14–15	June 7	Mt 18:21–22	Mar 16

Verse Used	Date	Verse Used	Date
Mt 19:23–24	Aug 17	Mk 5:34	Feb 3
Mt 20:12–16	Aug 18	Mk 6:12	Feb 5
Mt 20:14–15	Sept 18	Mk 6:17,27	Feb 6
Mt 20:21	Mar 10	Mk 6:34	Jan 4
Mt 20:27–28	July 28	Mk 6:45–46	Jan 7
Mt 22:17–21	Oct 16	Mk 6:56	Feb 9
Mt 23:11	Mar 9	Mk 7:6	Feb 10
Mt 23:12	Aug 20	Mk 7:21–22	Feb 11
Mt 23:25	Aug 25	Mk 7:34–35	Feb 13
Mt 24:42	Aug 26	Mk 8:8	Feb 14
Mt 25:20	Mar 29	Mk 8:34	Nov 26
Mt 25:22	May 9	Mk 10:14	May 21
Mt 25:35	Mar 11	Mk 12:30–31	June 2
Mt 25:37	May 13	Mk 16:15	Apr 17
Mt 25:35	Jan 19	Mk 9:4	May 16
Mt 25:40	Jan 25	Lk 1:28	Dec 8
Mt 26:15–16	Apr 7	Lk 1:30	July 26
Mt 28:5–6	Mar 26	Lk 1:38	Apr 4
Mt 28:19	May 22	Lk 1:39–40	May 31
Md 1:2–3	Dec 4	Lk 1:42–43	Dec 12
Mk 1:15	Jan 12	Lk 1:46–49	Aug 15
Mk 2:3–4	Jan 16	Lk 1:57–58	June 24
Mk 2:14	Jan 17	Lk 2:10–11	Dec 25
Mk 2:17	Jan 15	Lk 2:29–32	Dec 29
Mk 4:5–6	Jan 24	Lk 2:34–35	Sept 15
Mk 4:8	Jan 28	Lk 2:48	June 19
Mk 4:21	Jan 27	Lk 3:21–22	Jan 11
Mk 4:39	Jan 29	Lk 4:8	Feb 29
Mk 5:19	Jan 31	Lk 4:24	Aug 31

Verse Used	Date	Verse Used	Date
Jn 13:14–15	Mar 24	Acts 14:27	May 11
Jn 14:1	May 7	Acts 13:47–48	May 8
Jn 14:6–7	Apr 22	Acts 18:9–10	May 6
Jn 14:8	May 3	Acts 20:25	May 10
Jn 14:12	Apr 24	Acts 23:11	May 27
Jn 14:27	Apr 26	Rom 1:16	Oct 11
Jn 15:5	May 12	Rom 2:9–10	Oct 12
Jn 15:1–2	Apr 28	Rom 7:18–19	Oct 21
Jn 15:12–13	Apr 30	Rom 8:15–17	Oct 26
Jn 16:32	May 23	Rom 8:28	July 24
Jn 18:25	Jan 23	Rom 8:30	Sept 8
Jn 19:5–6	Mar 25	Rom 8:31–32	Oct 27
Jn 20:16–17	July 22	Rom 8:35	July 31
Jn 20:18	Mar 30	Rom 11:33–36	Aug 21
Jn 20:21	Apr 18	Rom 12:2	Nov 17
Jn 20:25	July 3	Rom 15:18	Nov 4
Jn 21:17	May 28	1 Cor 3:3	Sept 2
Acts 1:8	May 15	1 Cor 3:16	Nov 9
Acts 1:9	May 5	1 Cor 4:1	Sept 3
Acts 2:1–4	Jan 30	1 Cor 9:24	Sept 10
Acts 2:17	Apr 12	1 Cor 10:16	Sept 11
Acts 2:24	Mar 28	1 Cor 10:16–17	May 29
Acts 2:42–44	Apr 3	1 Cor 15:10	Sept 16
Acts 6:8–12, 7:58	Dec 26	2 Cor 4:5	Sept 13
Acts 8:30–31	Apr 29	2 Cor 4:7	June 10
Acts 10:37–38	Jan 9	2 Cor 5:1	July 27
Acts 11:26	Apr 19	2 Cor 9:6	Aug 10
Acts 13:45	May 2	2 Cor 9:7–8	June 15